AN OBSCURE PHILANTHROPIST

FRANK MATHEWS 1871-1948

Tony Rees

ISBN 978-0-9561775-0-6

Monograph #1 of the Institute for the History and Work of Therapeutic Environments

Published by   Castle View Books
                    PO Box 154
                    Ludlow
                    SY8 9BH

Printed by   Orphans Press
                    Leominster
                    HR6 8JT

ACKNOWLEDGEMENT

I am grateful for the help I received from the staffs of the Birmingham Central Library, the Guildhall Library and the Wellcome Library and the Record Offices and Local History Centres at Dolgellau, Lichfield, Ruthin and Smethwick. Thanks also to Dr Craig Fees, Archivist of the Planned Environment Therapy Trust, who read an early draft and pointed out, among other things, the possible significance of Frank's interest in the work of Edward Carpenter. Christine Mackreth and Rebecca Rees worked hard to rescue me from obscurities, repetitions, and grammatical slips and suggested important improvements to the shape of the book.

I have to thank the authors and publishers of "Bournville", "A Breath of Fresh Air", and "The Edwardian Lady" for permission to quote extracts. Full details of these works are given in the bibliography.

Frank's own writings are still in copyright and will be for another nine years and this book would be pointless without extensive quotations from them. I am not sure who owns the copyrights but I have contacted as many of Frank and Evelyn's residuary heirs as I can find and have to thank Jenny Carruthers, Catherine Sandbach-Dahlstrom and Nick Stevens for their permissions. If anyone else who may have a claim sees this I shall be glad if they will get in touch so that I can apologise and put things right.

This book would not have been started if my mother, Hilda Rees (nee Price), had not understood the importance of Frank's life and work and had not kept key documents, including his letters to her, and added her own summaries of events and if my father Leslie Rees had not cheerfully put up with it all.

CONTENTS

FOREWORD

Powered by the might of industrialisation, late nineteenth-century Britain was the wealthiest nation in the world. Its manufactures and financial services dominated the global economy just as much as its merchant fleet and Royal Navy dominated the oceans and its army and civil servants dominated an empire upon which the sun never set. Britain was at the apogee of its power and influence because of wondrous riches. In the 100 years from 1800 the national income had increased an amazing eight times while the population had only multiplied itself by four. This led to a marked increase in the share of wealth for each person – at least in theory.

There can be little doubt that the upper and middle classes had profited from industrialisation, along with a minority of the working class; but as the nineteenth century waned it became shamefully obvious that the working class in general had not gained as much as had the landed elite, merchants, manufacturers and shopkeepers. Even if the standard of living of the working class had improved in absolute terms, it was apparent that it had not done so in relation to the expanding assets of Britain. Glaring inequalities persisted and poverty continued unabated in the wealthiest country in the world. As an American, Henry George, put it in 1879, this dreadful paradox was 'the great enigma of the times'.

His book, Progress and Poverty was sub-titled An Inquiry into the Causes of Industrial Depressions and of the *Increase of Want with Increase of Wealth. The Remedy*. It gained wide publicity and set off fierce discussions. George highlighted the contradictions and unfairness of English society. These features continued to strike writers who were concerned with social matters. In 1905, L. G. Chiozza Money wrote *Riches and Poverty*. He was an avowed proponent of a radical redistribution of wealth by means of 'substituting public ownership for private ownership of the means of production'.

Money believed his researches underlined an unjust economic system.

He detailed how the aggregate income of the forty-three million inhabitants of the United Kingdom was approximately £1,710,000,000. Out of this one and a quarter million rich people took £585 million; those who were comfortable numbered three and three quarters million and had £245 million; whilst there were thirty-eight million citizens who were poor and who took £880,000,000. Money did not diminish the advancements that had been made in the lives of the working class. Overall there had been an increase in their wages as much as there had been a rise in the purchasing power of money, whilst the death rate had lowered. Still, Money's conclusion was stark: 'the position of the manual workers, in relation to the general wealth of the country, has not improved'.

The seriousness of the economic divisions in Britain and the prevalence of poverty impelled other writers to rail against an unfair society. Inspired by a mélange of motives that included fear, guilt, political ideology, Christian concern and humanitarianism, a few members of the middle class highlighted the 'Condition of England' question. Like the Fabians in 1884 those with a social conscience asked continually 'Why are the Many Poor'? And not only did they ask the question but often they sought to act for the common good and change society for the better.

Although the problems of poverty in London and especially in the East End drew most attention, there were also those in Birmingham who strove to help their less fortunate fellows. The Reverend T. J. Bass was the vicar of St Laurence, which covered Gosta Green and parts of Duddeston. It was one of the poorest parts of the city and he sought to alert the prosperous citizens of Birmingham to the plight of his parishioners with books such as *Everyday in Blackest Birmingham* (1898). The next year John Arthur Fellow, a socialist, called for the sweeping away of the worst housing in the city in a pamphlet *The Housing of the Poor*. Sadly it made little impact.

Then there were those who acted on the ground like Mrs Caswell. A middle-class woman she was a teacher of the Women's Adult School and was prominent in setting up the Floodgate Street Infant Welfare

Centre in about 1908. But importantly working-class people were not inert – they acted on their own behalf. One such person was Nurse Tucker. She had grown up poor in Deritend and after her husband died of TB she would have starved if it had not been for her neighbours. She herself then contracted TB but survived, afterwards vowing to devote herself to those who need her most – the poor of Deritend. Eventually qualifying as a midwife she worked out of Heath Mill Lane, next to Floodgate Street, succouring the ill and needy often without payment.

Another legendary figure locally was Ernie McCulloch, praised as the Prince of Beggars for the thousands of pounds he raised for good causes. He had also lived through hardships in his childhood and youth in Deritend and his desire to make life better for youngsters pushed him to become a speaker in the Bull Ring from 1903 and pull in money for the Royal Robins. Founded ten years previously by Mr Pentland, each summer this organisation took over 3,000 poor kids for a day out to Sutton Park.

Ernie McCulloch went on to work as a volunteer with various charities until he died in 1964. Loved as the 'kindest man in Birmingham' he had much in common with Frank Mathews. Although Frank grew up middle class he was as much affected by the debate about poverty amidst progress as was any working-class activist and, like Ernie, Frank was dedicated to doing something positive for social welfare and social justice. Again in a similarity between the two men, Frank devoted his life to the well being of children, and one of his most important supporters, Hilda Price, came from Deritend as did Ernie.

What is different between the two is that Ernie left behind no writings of his own to tell us about himself and what motivated him and nor has he found a biographer. Fortunately, however, Frank's words and deeds have now been brought to a wider audience by Tony Rees. Sensitively and thoughtfully Tony has told Frank's story and in so doing has shed light not only on the 'obscure philanthropist' himself but also on the motivations of other middle-class men and women who believed like he did in a fairer and more just society. Too rarely do people like Frank reach out to us as rounded characters and too rarely can we truly appreciate their work and their legacies. Therein lies the importance of this biography. Frank Mathews made a difference. He changed lives and we can understand him, his calling and his work all the better thanks to Tony's assiduous research and thoughtful writing.

Professor Carl Chinn MBE

PREFACE

In 1984 Central Independent Television broadcast a series about Edith Holden, the Country Diarist, based on the book "The Edwardian Lady" by Ina Taylor. A viewer wrote to the station:

> "I would like to say how much my husband and I enjoyed watching 'The Diary of an Edwardian Lady'. I am particularly impressed by the part taken by Frank Mathews.
>
> As a little girl of seven he was my saviour in as much that the medical profession had given me up as incurable. Consequently Frank Mathews took me under his wing and organised that I went to live on a farm at Tenbury Wells. From there I went to Haseley Hall a house opened for invalid children. I feel that Birmingham should be very proud of him. He did so much for the poor and the sick boys and girls, he was such a wonderful kind man.
>
> I am a grandmother of 65 years and have 5 grandchildren and another one due shortly. I do thank God for this wonderful man, he did it all out of charity and his own unselfish love, kindness and devotion.
>
> There must be hundreds of men and women to thank the Holden family and Frank Mathews. The last time I saw Frank he came to my home and tears came into his eyes when he saw my new born baby girl. She's 44 now. To think that little 'sprat' of a girl could now be a mum through all his love and caring…"

Frank Mathews appears only as a minor character in "The Edwardian Lady" but the family had a great influence on his life , and he on theirs. He first met Arthur Holden in 1890. Holden supported Frank in his early charitable work and soon introduced him to his wife and children. He became a welcome visitor to their home and, in 1904, married Evelyn, Edith's youngest sister. After they were married Evelyn gave up a promising career as a book illustrator to help Frank in his work: other members of the Holden family contributed time and money to his causes.

They were not, by any means, alone. Frank's two sisters supported and took an active part in his charities for the whole of their adult lives. Others, people who he met in the course of his work were drawn to him and stayed with him, often for decades. Some continued to work voluntarily for his causes long after he died.

They all did as they did partly because of the rightness of what he did. But that alone does not explain the loyalty which so many felt toward him. Rather, it was his quality as a man that drew them to him, his passion, his energy and, above all, his human kindness.

This book, then, is an attempt to show what sort of person he was by telling his story, both private and public and, perhaps, make it possible to understand the difference he made to the world he found and how, and why, he did it.

* * *

Frank started his philanthropic work in the 1890's when the ideas that would lead to the modern concept of a welfare state were only just being developed. This was a time when the cities and larger towns of England were expressing their civic consciousness in many material ways but when provision for the needs of the poor beyond that provided under the Poor Law was regarded as a matter for the charity of individuals.

This charity was not lacking and there were serious efforts, for example through the Guilds of Help that were organised in many towns around the turn of the century, to organise and systematise it. But it was, consciously or not, something that the better off did for the poor, whether they liked it or not. It was not long before it was realised that the problems of poverty were beyond cure by charitable means and the state, however reluctantly, stepped in, the first faltering step being the introduction of old age pensions in 1908.

Frank was, by upbringing and education, if not in financial resources, a member of the charity giving classes. He was well enough connected and, had he chosen to do so, he could, no doubt, have soon enough made himself rich enough to join in their almsgiving. Instead he chose to give his life.

Almost from the beginning, however, he saw his work in terms not of hand outs from the rich but of organising things so that the needy, in his case sick children, could get what they needed. His first major charitable work was called, symbolically, the Crippled Children's Union and his first thought was what the children could, with help, do for themselves. He always asked families to pay what they could toward treatment. It usually was not much and he developed formidable campaigning skills to get the balance from the authorities and the charitable. As will become clear his approach was very successful.

* * *

I have known Frank Mathews all my life – though he died in 1948 when I was sixteen. My mother had worked for him for several years before she married: when she left to become a full time housewife he continued to keep in touch, writing to her and visiting us from time to time. She, meanwhile, continued to help with the activities of his charities.

My first memory of him was when I was about three or four. My mother told me that he would be coming and that he couldn't hear very well. He would sometimes allow his wind to escape, thinking, because he couldn't hear it, that there was no noise. I must do my best not to notice.

He duly arrived, immensely tall it seemed and dressed in a grey suit of some magnificent cloth that seemed to shimmer and ripple. On his breast pocket he wore a bakelite box which was connected by a wire to a thing in his ear – his hearing aid. It can't have worked very well for he did produce, quite without self-consciousness, and I, no doubt, did my best to do as I had been told.

During the war, when my younger sister was old enough to go to school, my mother returned to his office. At first she went for one day a week, mainly to help keep the finances in order, but later she became a full time employee and, eventually, succeeded him as Secretary of his last charity, the Birmingham Society for the Care of Invalid and Nervous Children.

She continued with this work, until the charity was wound up in 1979 by which time she was herself over seventy years old and had retired to Sussex.

The whole of our family was very much involved, in a variety of minor roles, with Frank Mathews' affairs. We knew what he did and we knew many of the people who worked with him. We helped with a multitude of events that combined fundraising with activities that brought together the helpers and the helped in a way that he had always seen as pivotal to the success that he undoubtedly enjoyed with his work

Although it seems to me to be true to say that I have known Frank Mathews all my life I did not, of course, know him for most of his. This means that in writing this book I have had to try to use both my own memories of his last years and what I have been told or have been able to find out. Most of what I have to say from now on will be drawn from documentary sources, his reports, his letters, his other papers and the papers of others who had something to say about him. But interspersed will be material that I remember or that I was told by my mother, as well as some from her notes and essays about him.

She very much wanted this biography to be written, though she might have felt that I have given her too prominent a role, and prepared summaries of what she could remember as well as translating – and that is not too strong a word – some of his handwritten letters. I have put her memories and mine in without attribution to aid the flow of the narrative, though I am glad to acknowledge her contribution. As always, she would, no doubt, have preferred to remain anonymous.

My mother says in one of her notes that Frank Mathews corresponded regularly with friends. Sadly, he seems to have kept almost nothing he received, only a few post cards. He wrote several dozen letters to her: they provide a unique insight into both his conscious thought and his unconscious attitudes. Nothing much else of his private correspondence has come to light though he left a lot of recognisable, if anonymous, material in the public reports of his work.

He read a lot and was familiar with the nineteenth century classics and with serious writers among his contemporaries. He also spent a lot of time reading political commentators with whom he felt in sympathy but who have, by and large, not stood the test of time. These figure in his letters to my mother and, no doubt in his other correspondence. I have not quoted much from these feeling that they don't add much to what can be learned about him from his deeds.

There can't be too many people left, more than fifty years after his death, who can remember him clearly, particularly in his private life. Because he valued my mother's contribution to his work and regarded her as a friend to be looked after, I saw quite a lot of him during the last part of his life and perhaps the things I remember will help to colour the picture of him as a man.

One technical problem has been to know what to call everybody. He was, of course, called Mr Mathews in our house, except when my father daringly referred to him as FM – which he often used as a signature. I have chosen to call him Frank and feel that I can be excused such familiarity because I am now about as old as he was when I knew him. His wife I can call Evelyn because she was my friend until I was in my thirties and I used to call her Evelyn then. This makes it easy for the rest of the characters, including my parents and myself, whom I can simply call by our names as would anyone who didn't know them.

* * *

This, then, is the story of a man who I was lucky enough to know and who did extraordinary things in my home city of Birmingham. He was without any sort of pretension. Though he knew many of the great and good of the city – who willingly supported him in his endeavours – he spent his working life with the poor and the sick. For more than fifty years he worked for children suffering from crippling diseases, bringing about the cure of thousands.

He was a well known and popular figure and always seemed to be looked on with favour by the local and sometimes the national newspapers. He was almost unbelievably energetic in applying himself to his work though he paid the price as he got older in exhaustion and pain. He had the greatest patience with those who needed it and very little with anybody else. Astonishingly, for one with no formal training in either medicine or social science, he was very well thought of by senior professionals in both fields. He invented, and put into practise, important innovations in the treatment of childhood illnesses.

I have tried to paint a picture of him as a man – interesting enough to his friends – as well as giving an account of his work – which, I hope will be interesting to a wider audience. His work was so central to his adult life, as well as being an outcome of his earlier years, that the two fit together very easily. Without his work, and that particular kind of work, he would have lived a life of complete frustration.

Finally, I believe, the book has to try to put some sort of value on his work. This is something that I cannot do properly. It would require the work of a committee of experts – a notion that would have horrified him – as well as a poll of as many as could be found of the people he helped. However, there are clues in what was said and written while he was alive and in the subsequent testimony of people like the woman I have quoted. I have tried to point out these clues as I have gone along.

Above all, though, this is a story that has to try to take in and extraordinary person who was, above all, an emotional and loving man, and something of the understandings, often intuitive, that he brought to his work, many of which, I believe, were well in advance of their time and perhaps can teach us something today.

1871 – 1893 EARLY YEARS

Frank's father and mother, Daniel Mathews and Lucy Mary Helen Solomon, were married at St Michael's Church in the parish of her parents, Handsworth, Staffordshire, on August 25th, 1869. He was 34, a bank manager, born in Stourbridge and living in the parish of St Bartholomew, Wednesbury, she was 23 and a spinster. Daniel's father, Paul Mathews, is described as a Gentleman, presumably meaning either that he lived without the need to earn money or that he belonged to one of the gentlemanly professions; Lucy's father, James Vose Solomon, as a surgeon.

The couple must have started their married life in comfortable middle class circumstances with Daniel already established in a career that would bring them, at the very least, a reasonable living. Daniel's bank, a branch of the Staffordshire Joint Stock Bank was one of only two banks in Wednesbury and Daniel would have occupied a position of respect in his community.

The 1871 census shows the couple living at 30 Market Place Wednesbury, Staffordshire, the address of Daniel's bank, with their infant son Arthur, Matilda Bullock, his nurse, and Eliza Bailey, general domestic servant. Frank was born a few months after the census. Daniel gives his address, on the birth certificate, as 34 High Street.

The family would seem, therefore, to have been living "over the shop" early in 1871 and to have moved to 34 Lower High Street at some point in the few months after the census. Most likely they did so either because they expected to need more room when the baby arrived or because the bank was about to be demolished to make way for the building, still partly occupied by a bank, that now fills its site. Number 34 is one of comparatively few houses in Lower High Street that existed at the time and are still there. It is a not particularly large early Victorian terrace house which had, at the time, a decent rear garden. It now houses a shop on the ground floor. It is only a few yards from Daniel's bank, which was at the junction of Lower High Street and Market Place, so Daniel did not have far to go.

Within six years the couple had three children, Arthur Daniel, born in 1870, Frank, born a year later, on 2 September 1871, and Pauline Lucy Mary, born in 1875. Lucy was pregnant for a fourth time and the family was living at "Bank House, High Street" when Daniel died of typhoid fever in March 1876. Their daughter Ethel Alice was born a later that spring.

Daniel's death left Lucy in an almost impossible situation. She had four children to look after, one of whom, Pauline, was handicapped by deafness either from birth or from an early age – her grandfather Solomon made special provision because of her handicap when he wrote his will in 1888. In 1880 Lucy had an income varying between £70 and £110 per year from a share of rentals which she supplemented by taking in "young ladies who are at schools in the neighbourhood of her house by which means she (had) hitherto in part, but not wholly, maintained herself and (her) children".

As a daughter of a middle class household she would not have expected to have to maintain herself and would not have been brought up with any qualifications for earning a living outside the home Within a couple of years she had secured an education for Arthur at Clifton, Gloucester.

The 1881 census shows her living in Handsworth close to her parents' home. She is 35 years old and head a household of nine persons, including her daughter Ethel, aged 4. She describes herself as a "Governess" and has living with her Annie Pedley, aged 25, also a Governess, a Domestic Nurse, a Cook, a Housemaid and four female boarders aged from 12 to 20 who are described as Scholars. Whether the term Governess means any more than that she regarded herself as being, in some sense in loco parentis for the scholars is not clear. It is hard to see why she would need an assistant for that so perhaps there was some educational activity going on.

Lucy's parents, no doubt, helped out – Pauline was with them on census night. Though comfortably off they were not rich and would not have been able to support her family in middle class comfort in addition to seeing to their own needs. Lucy was hardly in deep poverty. Indeed, she seems to have arranged her lifestyle so that she could continue to support an appropriate number of servants, but the chance of support and a decent education for her second son must have been something she felt she could not ignore.

In March 1880, she had petitioned "the Right Honourable, Right Worshipful and Worshipful the Governors of Christ's Hospital, London.... in your usual Charity to Widows, Orphans, and Families, who stand in need of Relief, to grant the admission into Christ's Hospital, of .... Frank Mathews, at the age of eight years and seven months, there to be Educated and Maintained among other poor children and instructed in the Christian Religion according to the principles, doctrine and discipline of the Church of England".

The petition was countersigned by William Randall, minister of the parish of Handsworth, his two churchwardens, and three other housekeepers of the parish who collectively certified that Frank was no foundling and was not maintained at the parish charge, that they knew of no alternative means for educating him and maintaining him, that they and his mother agreed to leave him at the disposal of the governors while he was at the Hospital and would be responsible for his discharge when he reached the age of fifteen or on the governors' demand.

The petition papers included his parents' marriage certificate, his birth certificate, a certificate of baptism and answers to enquiries that showed that Frank was generally healthy, apart from a slight long sightedness and astigmatism and a tendency to suffer from catarrh of the middle ear.

Lucy's petition was successful and Frank was admitted to the school by the Court of 26 May. He was "clothed" – entered the School - on 9th September just after his ninth birthday. He remained a pupil until his discharge, on behalf of his mother, on 17th December 1886 at the end of the term in which his fifteenth birthday took place.

He was admitted to the Christ's Hospital boys' preparatory school at Hertford. He would have stayed there until he was eleven or twelve and then would have moved on to the main School, then in the City of London on the site given at the foundation by King Edward VI in 1552.

The preparatory school shared the Hertford site with the girls' school which had hitherto not been highly valued by the governing body. At the beginning of the nineteenth century there had been only 18 girl pupils, the minimum number to meet the conditions of an important bequest. At about the time that Frank went there the governors started to think in terms of providing academic education for girls. Their numbers had risen to 85, aged between 12 and 15 and there was a plan to bring it to 200. For the first time it was decided to appoint experienced teachers to provide it: in 1875 there was an advertisement for a principal mistress who "must have a thorough acquaintance with all subjects embraced in an ordinary English education, together with French, Drawing and Instrumental Music".

When Frank went there the preparatory school had about 380 boys aged from 8 to 12. They came from all over the British Isles and what was then the Empire though there was none whose surname was not either Anglo Saxon or Celtic. The living in staff included the Headmaster, the Reverend John Bell aged 36, the Steward, the Beadle, one master and the Headmistress as well as a Matron and nurses for boys and girls.

However, in Frank's time the boys and girls schools were kept strictly apart, meeting only for prayers, not, it seems for reasons of decorum but more because of the different views still taken about the proper education of the two sexes.

The disparity between the treatment of boys and girls was just one of the issues that drew the attention of the Charity Commission, which was in the process of reviewing educational charities at the time, and Frank may well have benefited from the beginning of a series of improvements in the school as a whole which culminated in the move of the main school to Horsham a couple of decades later. One reform he will have benefited from was the decision that had been taken in 1878 to divide the school year into three terms with four weeks holiday at Christmas and Easter and seven weeks in the summer. For the preceding three centuries children would have been allowed only the occasional leave day: some would only have seen their families two or three times in the course of their school lives.

What Frank felt about all this is not recorded but is not difficult to imagine. He was a little boy who had not long lost his father and he was to be separated from his mother and his brother and sisters and put among strangers. Separation from the family at eight or nine years of age is still regarded as normal in some circles but the effect of the separation added to that of bereavement may have been responsible for the passionate sympathy with deprived children that characterised, indeed dominated, his later life.

He does not seem to have made much of a mark at Christs Hospital. The only papers that he kept are a report for the half year ending Christmas 1882, which may have been the last of his time in at Hertford, and a ticket for a concert in December 1886, the month when he left the main School. His average place in the Grammar School at Hertford was fourth out of 45 and in the Writing School twentieth out of 42. In both his conduct and diligence were marked as good and in the latter he was awarded the Scripture Prize. How he got on in the main School is not known.

* * *

Between 1890 and 1900 Frank kept notebooks in which he jotted things he wanted to remember. There are two of them, black cardboard covered books of the type carried by policemen, small enough to fit easily into a pocket. The first, and smaller, has entries from 1890 to 1892, the second, giving his address as Dartford Heath, Kent, has entries from May 8th 1892 until some time in 1900.

These notebooks contain information about his reading and about some of his day to day activities. Crucially, the larger one also contains a chronology, obviously written for some biographical purpose, giving details of what he regarded as key events in his life from the time he started at Christ's Hospital. The chronology seems to have been added to on several occasions. Entries for the period from 1880 to 1899 look as though they were all written at the same time and there appear to have been additions in 1922, 1923 and 1937, the last three representing significant points of change for him.

After he left school, according to the chronology, Frank went for two years to Denbigh, in North Wales, where his older brother Arthur was living. He left no account of what he did there and his presence is not recorded in any official record. There was no Mathews living in Denbigh at the time of the 1891 census so there is no obvious family connection. Since both Frank and Arthur had to earn a living it seems likely that they were employed, perhaps in one of the "banking and clerking" jobs that he mentions in his chronology.

The brothers left Denbigh in August 1888 and Frank went to live with his mother in Edgbaston, Birmingham. There he worked in a number of clerical jobs found, perhaps, with the assistance of his father's former colleagues but, unsurprisingly in view of his later career, he doesn't seem to have settled. The problem of what he was going to do for a living must have been difficult, there being little money to pay for further education or training but he must have shown some interest in horticulture for the next documentary evidence of his doings is one side of a correspondence between his mother and the firm of Thomas Hewitt and Company's Solihull Nurseries near Birmingham.

The first letter, dated 3rd June 1889, three months short of his eighteenth birthday, is an answer to what was clearly a firm enquiry:

"In answer to yours we shall be very willing to take your son to learn our business and if he has any inclination for horticulture he can soon make himself useful. We should not give any remuneration for the first six months, after that he would be paid according to his usefulness. We may say that he would have to commence from the bottom and work his way through every stage as that is the only way to get really practical knowledge. Should you decide to send him we shall be glad to hear at your earliest convenience.

The hours are from 6 – 6 in summer and during daylight in winter. But any slight alteration in the hours we can arrange without difficulty.

We are etc".

The Mathews were, by then living at 69 Gough Road, Edgbaston, an inner but middle class suburb about a mile from the centre of Birmingham. To get to his work Frank would have had to find his way across the inner city to Snow Hill station in the centre and take a train to Solihull, a journey of the best part of an hour overall. Presumably he preferred the prospect to clerking but he was not letting himself in for an easy life.

Three months later, at the end of September, his employers were commenting both on the improved state of his health and on the interest he was showing in his work. They did, however, have second thoughts about his employment terms:

"With regard to his staying on with us, we do not quite see our way to continuing on the same terms and we should prefer him to become an apprentice in the same way as other young men have commenced. Our terms being as follows and by which you will see that the whole of the premium is returned to the apprentice at the end of his term. Premium £30 …the term to extend over a period of 3 years…."

It seems that Lucy had no objection in principle to this change and the premium – apparently negotiated down to £20 – was duly paid, the apprenticeship having been deemed to have started from the day Frank joined the firm.

When he left Hewitts, he went to work, in May 1892, in Dartford Heath but stayed there only four months. What he was doing is not known but it fell before the date at which his chronology records that he "left horticulture" so, presumably he had a job that made use of his qualifications. His experience with Hewitts certainly left him with a love of gardening that he never lost but, as his notebooks show, even while he was completing his apprenticeship with the firm, he had understood that while horticulture might provide him with a living it would not give him all that he wanted from his life. By October 1893, aged 22, he had "abandoned horticulture" as a career.

While he was at Dartford he took advantage of his nearness to London to attend a number of lectures. On Friday 24th June he heard John Trevor speak on "The Labour Church" – an organisation that would, very soon, be the locus of the first phase of his life's work – and on Sunday 10th July Mrs Aveling on "International Labour". Later, after he left Dartford he heard Sidney Webb on "New Parliament" and noted a series of lectures by Graham Wallas, another early Fabian, on "The English Citizen".

On 19 June 1892 he records a reading of his palm by a Miss Martin, on 17 July a card reading by a Mrs Peck and, on 23 July, a fortune telling by 'Cheiro'. None of the readings show any great prescience but they seem to reveal that the questions of most interest to him at the time included his health, his prospects of marriage and the general direction of his career that he thought might include authorship.

What is more interesting is that he chose to keep the original of the palm reading. This document, more than a thousand words, makes detailed predictions of the events and chronology of his life and describes a number of women who will influence him. In some places it fits what actually happened very well. In some places a fit can be interpreted and in others it is plainly wrong. Frank seems to have believed that it showed evidence of the reader's ability to foretell events and was to refer to it in correspondence fifty years later.

* * *

In her biography of Edith Holden, author of "The Country Diary of an Edwardian Lady", Ina Taylor tells how Arthur Holden, Edith's father, came to Birmingham from Bristol in 1865. With a partner he bought a firm of paint and varnish manufacturers; within three years he was in sole control of the firm which was to continue in business for the better part of a century.

Birmingham in the mid nineteenth century was an attractive place for an ambitious businessman. It was expanding rapidly and had a wide variety of trades, supported by good access to raw materials and markets. As a relative newcomer in the ranks of the larger towns it was free of the guilds that could hamper enterprise elsewhere.

For Arthur Holden there was another attraction: Birmingham's relatively late achievement of corporate status meant that it had not suffered under a law that forbad non-conformist clergymen from living within five miles. Holden came from a family that held strongly to the Unitarian church and he found in Birmingham a place where Unitarianism had been flourishing for many years and was supported by prominent citizens including Joseph Chamberlain, the greatest political figure in Birmingham at the time.

Holden also held enlightened political views and found the radicalism of Birmingham congenial – he was elected to the town council in 1873 being described by the Birmingham Morning News as "a modest but able and intelligent councillor possessing literary ability of no mean order, and although not distinguished as an orator" finding "an excellent field of labour on the Free Libraries Committee of which as well as the Baths and Parks he is a member". He was later a member, with Joseph Chamberlain, of the Gas Committee, set up to investigate ways of setting up one of the many municipal enterprises that were to contribute so much to the later strength of the city.

He was a model employer, treating his workers with respect. In return he inspired loyalty among them and was later remembered affectionately by them. He had a strong personal interest in the arts and was a leading member of the Central Literary Association, which met to discuss and participate in a wide range of philosophical and artistic pursuits, for almost all his lifetime in the town.

But one of his most abiding passions, stemming from his strong religious and political views, was a desire to help those less fortunate than himself, particularly the poorest people of the Birmingham slums. This desire was held by many who belonged to the Unitarian persuasion, a list of whose members contains many noted philanthropists.

The Unitarian congregation in Birmingham was founded in 1692 following the passing of the 1689 Act of Toleration. In 1862 a smaller chapel in Moor Street, built in 1832, was replaced by the Church of the Messiah in Broad Street which continued in use until 1973. Meanwhile two Unitarian Missions had been founded in 1840 and 1846. The Hurst Street Mission, renamed the Peoples Hall in 1886, was led by its Missionary Mr W J Clarke. It held services, attended, it seems, by the Holdens but its functions also included a number of activities designed to alleviate the distress of the poor.

* * *

Returning to 1889, we have Frank Mathews, aged 18, intelligent, almost overly serious minded and possessed of a good education at a school which had a tradition of emphasis on service to the community. He had worked for four years in a series of conventional jobs that, obviously, held no great interest for him and was about to start a three year apprenticeship in a trade where skill, rather than thought, was of the essence.

For the next three years he was extremely busy. He worked from dawn to dusk at Hewitts on weekdays and probably on Saturday too and he read extensively. On Sundays at least part of his time would have been spent on religious observances.

His mother's family name suggests that Frank had at least some Jewish ancestry. Be that as it may, Frank himself was christened at birth and was brought up in the Church of England, at that time the denomination required for admission to Christ's Hospital. But by the time he reached eighteen it seems likely that he had at least started to consider other forms of religion.

Frank's journeys to the centre of Birmingham from his mother's Edgbaston home would have taken him daily within a few yards of the Hurst Street Mission on his way to the station to catch a train to Solihull and on his way home after work. Neither his work nor his reading gave him any opportunity for social life of a kind likely to appeal to a seriously minded young man: it is not surprising that the Mission, with is combination of good works, political liberalism, and the society of such people as Arthur Holden, was very attractive to him.

It seems likely that Frank joined the Mission as a result of his contact with the Holden family which is said to have commenced with his meeting Kenneth Holden, Arthur Holden's older son, on a train journey in Wales. Frank records having met his future father in law, Arthur Holden, in June 1890. At that time, Holden was also attending the Mission so it is probable that Frank too was attending the Mission more or less from the time he started his job with Hewitts

Holden was thirty five years Frank's senior, successful, well connected and highly principled. He would have found Frank's interests and views congenial and it would have been natural for him to encourage the young man. As time went on they were to form a deep and lasting friendship and Frank would become a habitual visitor to the Holdens' houses in Kingswood, some sixteen miles from Birmingham, and, later Dorridge, a few miles nearer the city. His developing friendship with the family would culminate in marriage, though not until 1904, with Holden's youngest daughter, Evelyn.

The Hurst Street Mission and his friendship with the Holdens helped to fill the gap in Frank's social life and gave him an outlet for his developing desire to help others in the community but it is clear that he also felt a need to build upon the education that he had received at school especially by exploring spiritual and sociological matters.

By June 1890 Frank was recording and commenting on his reading. His notes are not always legible – a characteristic that got worse as he got older - but the first half dozen books are "Looking Backward" – a 'socialistic novel', "Robert Ellesmere" by Mrs H Ward – 'novel with a purpose', "From Matter to Spirit", "Social Problems" by Henry George – 'Socialistic', "Poverty" by James Platt – 'anti socialistic' and "John Ward, Preacher" by Margaret Deland – 'novel with a purpose'.

He was, obviously, impressed by "Spirit Teachings" by "M A Oxon" and quoted one passage at length in his notebook, sic:

> "p. 257 Begin with self – the Flesh Conquer it so that you are no longer Have no appetite to passion to ambition so that self can be abnegated and the spirit can come forth from its hermit cell and live and breathe and act in the free scope of universal brotherhood. This is the first step. Self must be crucified and from the grave where it lies buried will rise the enfranchised spirit untrammelled and free from material clogs".

Strong stuff for an eighteen year old but, oddly that it now reads, it reflects an important strand in the whole of his later life.

His investigation of spiritual matters – "Miracles of Spiritualism" by J Cook, "Theosophical leaflets"- 'give one an idea of Re-Incarnation', "Confessions of a Medium" – 'Part truth, part his past folly' was interspersed with more reading from the mainstream – "By order of the king" by Victor Hugo – 'semi historical novel', "Circuit journeys" by Lord Cockburn – 'fairly interesting', "Redgauntlet" by Sir W Scott, "My experiences in Spain" address by D Fitzgerald – 'seem to be the same as most peoples', and so on.

In all, he records twenty five books read or looked at in 1890, his interest in spiritual matters running in parallel with concern for social issues. He makes no comment on the last book he read during the year, "Story of an African Farm" by Olive Schreiner but it was one that he later admitted to admiring greatly. Also toward the end of the year he read some "Fabian Tracts", the first of which had been published by the recently formed Fabian Society in 1884 and had attracted Bernard Shaw into the Society.

Frank was to buy the first bound volume of the Tracts – 1 to 43 - when it appeared in 1893. He had, presumably, already read some but he chose to highlight passages in one - Fabian Tract No. 7 "Capital and Land" published in December 1891. His markings suggest that he was particularly struck by the concentration of wealth in the hands of the few – "one two hundredth part of the population owns ten elevenths of the total area" – by the result that the many were excluded from the enjoyment of the countryside and the high proportion of the population in absolute poverty " One in five of Londoners dies in the workhouse, hospital or lunatic asylum; one in eight of the manual labor class is a pauper, or has been one".

He was to continue recording and commenting on his reading until the end of the decade. In 1891 he divided his attention fairly evenly between spiritual matters, including Spiritualism in the strict sense, and social and political affairs, the latter including the lives of Darwin, Mazzini, Carlyle and Cobden. During 1892 and 1893 his reading turns away from spiritual matters and he combines a continuing interest in social and political affairs with a broader reading of nineteenth century classics, biography and recent novels. He read "Walden", "Tess of the D'Urbervilles", Ibsen's "Norah", Garnett's "Life of Emerson", "Silas Marner" and "The Scarlet Letter", among others, interspersed with such as "The Cooperative Commonwealth" by Lawrence Growland, which he describes as 'very well written and exhaustive' "Condition of Labour" by Henry George, "The Revolutionary Spirit preceding the French Revolution" and "The World went very well then" by Walter Besant.

From 1895 to 1900, when his record breaks off, he read novels, mainly English, some biography and some poetry having decided, it seems, that he had absorbed sufficient political and religious ideas for the time being. For 1895 he records only twelve books. Half were classics; Daniel Deronda, The Cloister and the Hearth, Les Miserables, A

Russian Proprietor, The Cossacks and Hereward the Wake; the remainder were by contemporary novelists who have not survived.

In 1897, for example, he records twenty five books, all but three novels, including three by J M Barrie, five by Dickens and one each by Charlotte Bronte, Emily Bronte and George Eliot. The three non fictional works were a critical study of Shakespeare, a study of Walt Whitman and "Leaves of Grass" which he later said was one of his most loved books. At about this time he seems to have started his personal library by buying cheap uniform editions of authors he liked either en bloc or as they came out. His twenty five volume set of the Waverley Novels, for example, was published in 1886-7 and must have been bought together while his set of Thackeray was published in 1898-1900 at about the time he was reading them. He may well have borrowed Stevenson's novels from Evelyn Holden who was collecting an edition at the time he read at least some of them.

The change in his reading at about the year 1894, when he was twenty three, is mirrored by other changes in his life. As we shall see in the next chapter, this was when he set up in business as a shopkeeper and began what was to be his real life's business of helping poor and sick children. He may even have considered marriage. Though the shop keeping turned out to be a dead end and he did not marry at the time it does seem that the year 1894 marked his coming of age in the sense that he stopped preparing himself for what was to come and started his life proper.

1893 – 1897 THE CINDERELLA CLUB

At about the time that Frank records that he left horticulture he also states in his Chronolgy that he "Met Jeannie, October '93". Early in 1894 he bought and read three booklets, written by Edward Carpenter and published by the Labour Press Society, "Woman and her place in a free society", 6d, "Marriage" 6d, and "Sex-Love and its place in a free society," 4d. He kept them until he died.

The books themselves, as might be expected, do not go into detail about physical matters, though they must have seemed daring at the time setting out, as they do, a progressive position on the relationship that should obtain between men and women. Frank seems to have been most interested by the "Marriage" in which he marked several passages. But the fact that he chose to keep them suggests that they may represent some important node in his life.

In the absence of any other explanation, and knowing that Frank only recorded what he regarded as pivotal events in his chronology, it is tempting to put the two together as representing a love affair that, for some reason, he was unable to turn into a marriage. It is easy to imagine a scenario in which a couple might wish very much to marry but be prevented by the would be husband's lack of means and immediate prospects. Frustratingly though, no other evidence seems to exist.

Edward Carpenter was a fine scholar and a pivotal figure in the formation of the philosophy of the early socialists but he also wrote on a wide range of social and religious topics. He was a considerable poet and composer, writing, among other things, songs for the socialist movement. He was openly homosexual at a time when homosexuality was far from being tolerated and wrote extensively on the relationship between the sexes. Frank refers to him twice in his reading lists for the 1890s. As well as the three pamphlets mentioned above he read "England's Ideal", a collection of papers on social subjects, in 1894 but, sadly, he stopped recording his reading before the publication of some of Carpenter's most important works. Among these are "Adam's Peak to Elephanta", 1890, "Days with Walt Whitman", 1906, and "The Intermediate Sex", 1908, all of which will be seen to have influenced Frank throughout his life.

In the early 1890's Frank became a member of the Birmingham branch of the Labour Church, another of Carpenter's interests. We know that he had been at a lecture about the Labour Church in June 1892, while he was at Dartford, so perhaps he was inspired to make a local contact more or less as soon as he returned to Birmingham. It may have been that the Labour Church was where he first came across Carpenter's writings. Frank's involvement with the Church continued until 1915 at least: when he died he still owned a copy of its Hymn Book, published in that year.

A Statement of Principles on the back of the book's title page makes it clear that, while existing "to give expression to the religion of the Labour Movement", its respects whatever theological convictions its member may hold – in that it is not entirely unlike the Unitarians. It defines "the religion of the Labour Movement" as seeking "the realisation of universal well being by the establishment of Socialism – a Commonwealth founded upon Justice and Love".

The Labour Church was not the Labour Party whose beginning is usually said to be the formation of the Labour Representation Committee in 1900. But it was a political organisation dedicated to making things better on Earth and it is typical of him that Frank should soon seek to use it to do something about a pressing need that he, and others, could seek staring them in the face.

Frank was probably living in Birmingham at the time he met Jeannie and joined the Labour Church, though the direct evidence comes only from a later insertion in the Chronology. However, it is clear from an original entry that he "Started at Lichfield March 94" and "Left

Lichfield Dec 96". Elsewhere he gives his address as that time as Market Street, one of the main shopping streets in the centre of the town.

Lichfield is an ancient town about ten miles to the north of Birmingham. It is well known in history, among other things, as the site of a siege in the civil war in which its three spired cathedral was much knocked about and as the birthplace of Dr Johnson though by the end of the nineteenth century it had been dwarfed by its southerly neighbour. It was, however, more or less home ground for Frank with Wednesbury, his birthplace, only a few miles away among the Black Country towns to the West and Handsworth, where his mother's family still lived close by to the Southeast.

Kelly's Directory of 1896 records the firm of Mathews and Brooks, Seedsmen and Florists, at 34 Market Street: other records indicate that T W Brooks occupied the premises as a grocer from 1896, when Frank left the business. Thus it seems that, despite having "left horticulture" in October 1893 after his return from Dartford Heath, he was still hoping to use his horticultural knowledge to make a living.

While he was in Lichfield an event that was certainly pivotal in Frank's life took place. In itself it was not specially remarkable – a young man with time on his hands, and, possibly, recovering from a failed love affair, becoming involved in spare time charitable work. But it was the point at which he set out on the path that he was to follow for the rest of his days.

The day when he took the first step seems to have been November 15th 1894 when a meeting was held at the Birmingham Labour Church in Bond Street to discuss the forthcoming activities of the Cinderella Club. Those present were Thomas Bond (in the chair), a Mr Brown, Mrs Chickley, Miss Davis, Mrs Glazier, Thomas Groom, F. C. Humphries, G. H. (Hubert) Humphries, Frank Mathews, a Mr Muir, G. Saville, and a Mr Wellings. Thomas Bond was unanimously elected Treasurer and Frank Mathews Secretary.

"It was decided to hold the first Entertainment the following Thursday according to the following Program.

Children to arrive at 7.30 pm and to have two buns and two cups of cocoa. After that to have Games, songs and a fairy tale told them. At 8.45 Cocoa and a bun and an apple to go away with"

The record of the meeting is in Frank Mathews' handwriting, still, at this point, reasonably legible. It may be the first written evidence of the activities of the Club, though a printed report with the accounts of the "winter session", 1 October 1894 to 31 March 1895, says that "The Birmingham Labour Church Cinderella Club was started in November 1893".

The expenditure for that session was just over £24 of which £16/10s was spent on food, 11s on hire of crockery and £2/13s on hire of magic lantern and accessories. The income during the period came from donations and collecting cards.

The report, which is intended primarily as an appeal for money, sets out the principles, aims and activities of the Club:

"…..A commencement was made with about three dozen children between the ages of seven and ten, drawn from the poorest of poor districts. Recognising the fact that it is impossible to amuse – and the primary object of the Cinderella, let it be distinctly understood, is to amuse, and not to educate – children if their stomachs are empty, the first proceeding was to feed them (and this has been and is the invariable rule at all the gatherings). This is done somewhat as follows: Each child, on presenting his or her ticket (and these tickets, by the way, are distributed with great discrimination by the Masters and Mistresses at the various Board Schools) is given a large piece of cake and cocoa ad libitum. An inspection of the children's clothing is then made, and if any are badly in need of clothing – we very much regret to say that from 25 to 50 percent are greatly in need of clothes – their names are taken and handed over to the Police-Aided Clothing Scheme. After this the entertainment is proceeded with in earnest. The amusements are of a very varied character, consisting mainly, however, of a magic lantern, conjuring, nigger minstrel business, songs, etc. Sometimes the entertainments are interspersed with games, chosen chiefly by the children themselves – the most popular being those with good rollicking choruses. As the children are dispersed...."

It goes on to make it clear that the Committee members do not intend to limit the Club's activity to evening entertainments:

"....Can it be known that there are hundreds of children attending the schools in the slum districts of this city who have never been into the country? ....In drawing up our scheme for taking poor and destitute children into the country, we desire to say most emphatically that we do not dogmatise, or even attempt to teach the children, except to keep order, and to treat each other kindly. Our only object is to bring happiness into their lives....

....In conclusion, we appeal most earnestly for funds to take these little ones into the country, at least once a year, that they may hear the birds sing, and breath fresh air, and learn that there is something more beautiful than the filthy rooms and streets in which they dwell. We estimate that about 35/- will take a party of 50 children to Sutton, and provide them with a good meal when there. We have a good staff of workers; we only require the funds".

This, and other, fundraising activities had some success, income rising to £72 in the third year (1895-96) and £148 in the fourth. Most of the income in both years came from donations, almost all of a pound or less.

These paragraphs give some sort of idea of the living conditions of the poorest in the city, conditions that are hard for us to imagine not much more than a hundred years later. At the end of the nineteenth century the only safety net was provided by the poor law which condemned those who could not support themselves to workhouses whose regime was deliberately made so unpleasant that anyone who could possibly do so stayed out of them.

At times of national prosperity things were bad enough, with wages for an able bodied but unskilled man barely sufficient to keep a family fed and housed. As a result, families turned to secondary incomes, sometimes the few pence per week that could be earned by a child looking after infants for a working mother or selling matches in the street – barely removed from begging from the passing middle class. At times of recession the unskilled readily became the unemployed and general poverty became acute with children undernourished and often clad, literally, in rags.

There were, of course, many among the more prosperous who knew about and deplored these conditions. There were many who tried to help the poor through charitable social work and there were those among the enlightened of all political parties who saw the need for reform and tried to do something about it – slum clearance and the provision of decent housing, social security support for the old and unemployed, health care for all – but political reform took a long time, the whole of the twentieth century some might say, and in the mean time the conditions were as they were.

The only way they could quickly be made more tolerable was by means of charitable acts by those who could afford to perform them. By and large, people, particularly the most successful, do seem to have been willing to give money even if not on the scale that they give it now through taxation. But turning money into help also required people willing to give up their time and the Cinderella Club was the first means by which Frank Mathews started to give his time, and eventually his whole life, to help the poor and sick.

The Birmingham Labour Church was not the first Labour Church to start a Cinderella Club. The idea seems to have started in Manchester, probably in 1890, and by 1893 there were clubs in eight northern and midland towns and the Labour Church Institute in Manchester was starting to publish "Cinderella, A Paper for Cinderella Children" as a supplement to its "Labour Prophet".

But to return to Birmingham in 1896.

The third year's report of the club also contains an announcement that was to have resonances in Frank's future, both personal and professional. It is of…."a cottage at Kingswood, kindly lent to us for April, May and June, by Mr A Holden. This we have roughly furnished and have installed a caretaker, and are sending batches of four children (boys and girls alternately) for a fortnight's stay, and the good simple food and pure air, works marvels on these poor little mites, who are the most needy little invalids we can find in the slums of Birmingham. It would hardly be possible to send these if we had not our own cottage, as people in the district will not board these very sickly little waifs because of the care they need. They are so poor that clothes have to be found them before they go…."

The idea of taking children away from their terrible living conditions for periods of recuperation represents a significant development in Cinderella Club thinking and the fact that the cottage at Kingswood came from Arthur Holden, Frank's friend, suggest that it was Frank who was pushing the development along as his own ideas evolved.

The report of the fourth year's work summarises achievements to date:

"During 1893-94 we fed and amused about 1,000 children in the winter, and took 100 children out to the country in two parties in the summer of 1894. In the winter of 1894-95 we fed and amused about 2,000. In the summer of 1895 we took 400 out to the country in eight parties. During the winter of 1895-95 we fed 5,200, and in the summer of 1896 took 400 out to the county in eight parties as before. This last summer, in addition to the outings, we entertained 35 poor little invalids at a cottage in the country (kindly lent us by our friend Mr Holden), for a fortnight at a time. During last winter we fed and entertained over 7,000 children."

The first report is signed by all the officers and the second by Frank Mathews as honorary secretary, giving his Lichfield address. The third he signs as "Retiring Hon Secretary" for he had, by then moved on to other things. He was, however, to remain as Honorary Cottage Secretary for a further year.

Following Arthur Holden's loan of a cottage in the summer of 1896 – the Holdens moved away from Kingswood in 1897 - the Committee rented a cottage at Streetly, near Sutton Coldfield which they were able to keep open for six months in 1897 and seven months in 1898. Writing in the sixth year's report (1898-99) Frank gives some details of a few of the children who went there:

"Alfred – Age 10 years. Both knees diseased for nearly four years. Blind in one eye. One of four children. Father a nail maker, been out of work a long time.

Leonard – Age 14 years. Hip disease. One of four boys. Father dead.

Harriet – Age 12 years. Badly paralysed. Father been dead eleven years. Mother works at hinge making.

Harry – Age seven years. One leg taken off, been under seven operations. Mother a widow.

Lily – Age 8 years. Very bad state of health, bad body sores. Has a sister with spinal trouble. Father ill in infirmary. Mother very delicate."

These descriptions give some sort of idea of the terrible conditions that the children were living in, ill fed, clothed often in rags and living in overcrowded and verminous houses. As an indication of the concrete benefits from even a short stay in good condition Frank gives half a dozen examples of weight gain. The greatest gain was 7.5 lbs in three weeks, the least, 2 lbs over two weeks and the average just over 4 lbs (2 kg). The less concrete results he describes as "immeasurable".

They are also among the earliest examples of a technique he was to continue with throughout his working life of giving examples, made suitably anonymous, of the children his subscribers were helping , thus making both the need and the benefit more vivid to the subscriber.

They also link this work with the next phase of Frank's life for it must have been his involvement with the Cinderella Club that opened his eyes to the needs of poor crippled children in the City.

Frank does not seem ever to have belonged to a political party or to have campaigned actively in the political arena but it is evident from his early reading that his sympathies lay with the socialists of the day. Nor was there any inconsistency in his simultaneous adherence, at that time, to the Unitarians, for the British Labour movement had its roots as much in non-conformist Christianity as in the Trade Union movement. Its theorists were the social reformers of the Fabian Society, rather than followers of Marx, but, although he read the Fabians' work and agreed with their objectives, there is no evidence that he felt inclined to get involved with changing society by political means.

Rather, he felt an immediate compulsion to do something to alleviate the suffering that resulted from the conditions that he hated. This was most obvious in his early work for the Cinderella Club but, even as he later developed ways of understanding and dealing with problems that came largely, but less obviously, as a result of social conditions, he was to continue to concentrate his efforts on reducing suffering. The Cinderella Club reports underline the purpose of alleviating suffering, in their case through healthy activity, and they specifically reject education and dogmatisation – not that the Labour Church was a particularly dogmatic organisation. Frank himself held strong views all his life about politics and, for at least his first fifty years, about religion. But his work with the Cinderella Club is typical of his life as a whole. He saw it as a way of applying his beliefs, not of spreading them.

It is remarkable how rapidly the Cinderella Club developed while he was its secretary. He was working, unpaid, in his spare time while earning his living elsewhere so he cannot have been solely responsible for the rate of growth in the scale of what was done but there is a change in approach, from simple entertainment, through day trips to the country to longer stays with emphasis on long term benefits to the worst off that seems likely to have owed much to his influence. The last emphasis transfers directly into the next phase of his career.

Frank had lived in Denbigh for some time in his late teens, possibly staying with his older brother Arthur. The town is in the Vale of Clwyd, in North eastern Wales and is surrounded by ranges of open mountain moorland from which all the mountains of Snowdonia can be seen. Although it was then in a coal mining area, it must, even then, have been a surpassingly beautiful place to live. It may have been this first exposure to mountain scenery that sowed the seed that was to develop into a love of hill walking that was to last the rest of his life.

Later on, even into his seventies, he would roam on his own over the highest mountains of North Wales. This was much against the advice usually given to walkers at the time but he got to know the mountains so well that he was unlikely to get lost or wander into dangerous ground. He claimed that he was so relaxed that he never hurt himself when he fell. At any rate, he never did come to any serious harm.

The earliest evidence of this developing passion is that, in 1895 he joined a party, organised by the National Home Reading Union, on a holiday at Barmouth a seaside town on Cardigan Bay on the West coast of Wales. Barmouth stands at the mouth of the beautiful Mawddach estuary and looks across it to Cader Idris on the southern edge of what is now the Snowdonia National Park. It is reached by main road from Dolgelly, at the eastern end of the estuary and by rail by a line along the coast that originates in the English midlands. It makes an excellent centre for mountain holidays in this southern part of the park.

The programme for this week long holiday, which he kept, shows the participants arriving for a 6.30 dinner on Saturday and, after a 1.0 pm Sunday dinner, a Service at the Panorama Walk with a collection to help provide holidays for the slum children of Manchester, Liverpool and London.

The serious business of the holiday started on Monday with a twelve mile climb to the top of Cader Idris, 2,949 feet high, to hear a lecture on the "Old Glaciers of N. Wales" by the Reverend Z Mather.

Tuesday's excursion started with a train ride to Harlech to see the castle followed by a journey by narrow gauge railway and a five mile walk. On Wednesday there was no organised activity and on Thursday there was another long walk with a talk, this time the talk was on the flowers of the mountains and moors by the guide, Mr E D Jones MA. The holiday finished gently with a carriage drive and a three mile stroll to see the falls of Pistyll Cain and Rhaidr Mawddach, just north of Dolgelly.

One of the local secretaries for the holiday centre was T Arthur Leonard, a Congregationalist minister and a notable pioneer of active holidaymaking in the countryside. He and Frank may not have met on this occasion but they would certainly have done so during the week from July 24th 1897 when Frank acted as financial secretary and Leonard as local secretary for a holiday organised jointly by the Union and the Cooperative Holidays Association at Min y Mor, in Barmouth.

Leonard had started the Cooperative Holidays Association in 1893 having discovered that few of his congregation at Colne, Lancashire had any experience of the countryside, and was, in 1897, its general secretary. Like Frank he was greatly concerned with helping the very poor. The holiday party Frank attended was invited to contribute to the cost of holidays for the poor, the printed programme of the holiday including details of what had already been done that are reminiscent of some of the details in the Cinderella Club's reports. Frank Mathews and Arthur Leonard were clearly of similar minds in many ways and remained friends for the rest of their lives.

As for the holiday in Barmouth in 1897, participants were bidden to arrive on the Saturday for High Tea, from 6.0 to 8.0 pm. On Sunday afternoon, as on the previous occasion, there was a Service on the Panorama Walk and a collection – Frank collected £1 .3. 6d to be divided equally between the Fresh Air Fund for London and the

Provinces and the Association for Providing Free Holidays for Poor Folk.

The remainder of the programme was similar to that of 1895 except that the climb of Cader Idris was delayed until the Tuesday, presumably to break people in gently. Even with that precaution "those friends unable to keep up with the main party" were urged to abandon the climb altogether lest "delay and anxiety" be caused. Frank made another collection at the end of the week, raising £1 .4. 6d for the staff gratuity fund.

Frank took a similar holiday at Bangor in July 1898, again acting as financial secretary to Leonard's local secretary. In 1899 he spent two weeks at Portrush in Northern Ireland, acting as local secretary for the first week and financial secretary for the second.

It is obvious that here, as in other aspects of his life, Frank did not do things by halves. If he was to have the benefits of the holidays he was prepared to commit himself in advance to the effort of helping organise them. But by the time his interest in the mountains had established itself in this way he had already moved on to the next stage of his working career.

1897 – 1899 MISSIONARY

On March 12th 1897 Mr W J Clarke, Missionary at the Birmingham Unitarian Domestic Mission in Hurst Street wrote to Frank as follows:

"Dear Mr Matthews (sic)

I think that you will be glad to learn that the Committee have this evening unanimously decided to ask you to become my assistant for an experimental period of three months at a salary of 30 shillings per week.

It would suit me best to commence in the first week in April next. If however you particularly wish to start earlier I daresay it could be arranged.

I will write you in the course of the next day or two and make an appointment when we can talk the whole matter carefully over.

Sincerely do I hope that this may be the beginning of our permanent and mutually satisfactory association.

Sincerely yours

W J Clarke"

A formal confirmation from W H Ryland, Secretary of the Mission, came a few days later.

Frank was, by now in his mid twenties and knew, pretty well, what he believed and what was important to him and was close to finding his life's work.

His formal education at Christ's Hospital would have been permeated by an ethic of service to the community which was reinforced by his later self education. His choice of reading, and his comments on it, show how he had come under the influence of the radical thinkers of the left and that this had led to an early commitment to socialistic ideals coupled with an interest in religious ideas. The conditions in which poor people lived appalled him, his empathy being all the stronger because of his own childhood experiences. His record with the Cinderella club had already shown how hard he was prepared to work to do something practical to help people, and especially children, who needed it.

He had tried several ways of making a living – he had neither capital nor much in the way of expectations – but none had appealed to him. "Banking and clerking" are dismissed in his notebook without comment, horticulture, although he was to remain a keen gardener all his life, did not, it seems, offer a sufficient challenge, retail trade either did not prosper or did not enthral him.

When a possible opportunity came up of being paid, however modestly, to do what he felt most impelled to do he took it.

As well as his letters from Mr Clarke and Mr Rylands Frank kept one from R F Martineau an early supporter of the Cinderella Club and, at that time, a city councillor. It was dated March 10th 1897 and referred to Frank's "present application". It goes on:

> "I have much pleasure in testifying to your earnestness and ability in work for the poorest among our city children.
>
> I have seen with interest and admiration your devotion to the welfare and enjoyment of the poor little things. I know how care for them has been the motive of your life for some years past; and I can imagine no greater help than the enthusiasm which you would bring to bear among the children in his neighbourhood."

Mr Clarke would have, in any case, been well aware of Frank's interest and of his record with the Cinderella Club. The Club worked closely with the Mission over the provision of clothing for the most needy and Unitarians, including Arthur Holden, had been supporters from the start. But it does not seem that he knew him well personally – he addressed him formally even though Frank was a much younger man and he spelt his name wrongly using the more common form – or that the appointment had been discussed in detail in advance. The reference by Mr Martineau to an "application" even suggests the possibility that the job was not necessarily created with Frank in mind.

The Hurst Street Mission had been founded in 1840, one of a number established in major cities around England to "enlighten the ignorant and reform the vicious, and seek and save that which is lost".

In its early days a great part of the Hurst Street Mission's effort was devoted to providing elementary education for the poor but this activity was discontinued after the passage of the Elementary Education Act in 1870. For this and other reasons, the affairs of the Mission had, by 1885, become very much depressed and the Committee even considered its closure but, in the end, it was decided to continue and Mr W J Clarke was appointed Missionary.

He worked energetically and successfully to turn the Mission round and, within five years it was thriving again with a wide range of activities, religious and secular. Many of the latter were concerned with supporting the hard up; a savings club and a provident institution to help to smooth out the worst economic ups and downs, home visits and a relief fund for the distribution of medical notes, garments, money, coals, and food.

When he joined the Mission as Mr Clarke's assistant seven years later Frank would have had no difficulty in finding something to do.

It seems that he was required, from time to time at least, to give the address at Sunday Services. Several of the texts of these addresses survive: it is obvious that they were intended as notes: they are written in pencil or ink on scraps of paper, two being on the backs of two of the others. There are eight of them: six are original texts and two are reworkings of two of the others. This suggests that he kept all that he ever produced and that he was only required to give an address two or three times a year.

Sometimes his thinking outpaced his pen and the manuscripts only make complete sense with a certain amount of editing. This has been done in the quotations below. The underlinings are his.

He used them to set out his own ethical and moral positions. For example, on the text "He who findeth his life shall lose it and he that loseth his life shall find it" he wrote, in September 1898, or thereabouts,…

"We are so absorbed in obtaining our living that we often forget the purpose of our existence and as we devote Sundays to a halt in the march for a living, I choose today to consider what we live for and whether we are attuning to it. Firstly, we admit that life is eternal, that death is a mere dropping of the shell, that the self continues…then we say there must be a God and that we owe him a duty…to approximate ourselves to Him as nearly as we can…

The chief characteristics which make Christ stand out as one whose example is worthy of imitation are his perfect self sacrifice, his pity, his great love for all, his forgiveness of those who wronged him and his simplicity. Are our lives based on these virtues…?

Let us consider firstly Christ's pity, we must all of us know that around our homes and in our streets there is a vast mass of uncomforted poverty, of vice, crime and degradation. What are we ourselves doing, we who call ourselves followers of Christ? We say "what a pity that it should be so". Is this pity do you think? Perhaps we give what we can spare toward the relief of suffering but is this the pity of Christ? No indeed for Christ denounced the rich, but we cannot for we acquiesce in the system which permits the existence of vast riches in one place and vast poverty in another. We shall not prove our pity till we have determined to find out why poverty and misery ((exist)) and how they can be done away with and have set ourselves to the task of doing away with them.

One of the first steps to be taken is to admit that the rostrum and pulpit are the right places for social questions to be spoken of ….If every pulpit in the land today was ringing with the terrible cry of the lead workers, who are being poisoned and blinded and deprived of the boon of bearing healthy children because their employers say that they cannot afford to use a non poisonous glaze for their pottery, in three months time the poisonous glazes would be done away with......Is not this work for followers of the great Master to do?"

Is not the pulpit the right place to ring out the cry of the children who are being morally and physically ruined by working as half timers in the factories of Lancashire, Yorkshire and elsewhere. We are Christians, we say, and yet we pass daily in our streets children who are partially clothed and filthily dirty and aged people whose condition shows that theirs is an almost dishonourable old age. And if we be really followers of the Master we must not blame, merely the parents and relatives, for, if we enquire dispassionately, we shall find that their condition was neglected, that they have become degraded and brutalised by living in houses which are ugly and streets which are mean and, often unhealthy, that they know nothing of recreation which would have elevated them and their children. Are they to blame? Surely not, but we are for not finding out the why and wherefore....

Another point in the gospel of living for the sake of life is the great need for a universal love in place of our almost universal doctrine of doubt and mistrust of our fellows. Can it be said of a nation that it believes in love when it owns a Poor Law system such as ours. We pretend that we do not like the poor to starve when they become old or prematurely infirm and we send a class of people to be Guardians of the Poor who have no conception of the fact that love is a duty they owe to those unfortunate enough to come under their care. They have produced a system so cruel in most places that thousands would rather starve, and do starve, rather than accept the loveless hospitality which the state provides for them.

I know there is a slight improvement in the system, but in Birmingham, where we have a comparatively humane Board, I have, in only 18 months experience of Mission work come across many tragedies which might have been prevented, without any serious costs to the rates either, but (by) love and pity for the poor. But love and pity are the last thing the average Guardian of the Poor thinks of and we are responsible for we send the Guardians there to represent us….."

The address goes on with an illustration from a literary allegory and an explanation of how people must change individually if the condition of society is to alter. The appeal is in Christian terms though the objectives are political in the spirit of William Morris and Edward Carpenter, his point being that politics must become ethically based and that it is up to individuals to make them so.

We can make what we will of the outward purpose of the address and its likely impact upon his audience but there can be no doubt about his passion nor about the sincerity of his disgust about what he saw about him. Many of the evils he describes have, a hundred years later, either disappeared or been much ameliorated by political action, the latter often inspired by the values he advocated – though others may have taken their place.

When it came to it, though, Frank could not bring himself to wait for the world to improve. He had to do what he could to ease suffering straight away.

He had already been doing so, of course, through the Cinderella Club. The reports of the Club, as we have seen, show how Frank was coming into contact with children with bodies terribly damaged by illnesses brought on by their living conditions. He must also have known before he got the job in the Mission that there were a group of members who were starting to do something to help crippled children – he may even have been a member of that group.

When he arrived as Missionary it would have been astonishing if he had not wanted to put his weight behind its work.

One of his addresses, "Crippled Bairns", briefer than the others, shows us how much this need was most on his mind:.

"Life for the poor is nowadays very intense. Their bread is never quite certain, the breadwinner may be struck down by illness or work may grow slack and 'then what shall we do?' I think many of the workers may have this thought constantly in their minds and this intensity affects the children of the poor for as soon as they can be of the slightest use they have to begin to help on the ordinary routine of the house.

It begins with minding the baby as soon as they are 6 or seven years old and then it comes to running errands and fetching the coal and this is followed, often, by selling matches or newspapers and, in the case of little girls, often, as soon as school is over they have to go and mind a neighbour's baby for 2d or 3d per week.

All this tends to make the children of the poor old before their time and, if it affects able bodied bairns how must it affect the crippled ones. This is what we have to consider today, what the life of a crippled child belonging to poor parents is and how we can alter it.

Let us for a moment consider what it means to be crippled. A child is playing in the road and gets run over by a van and the leg is so smashed it has to be taken off. Henceforth ((the child)) must go on crutches for years and then, if it has good friends it may obtain a wooden leg. But, after all, that is poor compensation for the real one.

Or perhaps the mother has had to go to work and leave the children to be minded by a child and one has a heavy fall. No harm seems to be done at the time but in a few weeks or, in some cases months, the child limps and feels pain in the hip or knee and is taken to hospital. The doctor pronounces it to be hip disease which, perhaps most of you know can only be cured in two years under the most favourable circumstances and may mean, and usually does for the child of the poor, 4 or 5 years of suffering. And, if the disease takes the bad form and abscesses develop, the child, in a great many cases, becomes a chronic invalid with only a small hope of recovery and the certainty of years of pain and no hopes of ever being able to earn its living at any rate in the ordinary ways.

The fall may lead to hip ((disease)), as I have seen, or it may lead to, what seems to me to be worse, Spinal disease, for this not only cripples its victims but deforms them as well making them humped backed. Here too, if the dreaded abscesses form there is little or no hope of the child ever becoming an effective worker for its only hope of life is to lie on its back always. And if its parents cannot force it to lie down the child will slowly but surely die.

Then there are the paralytic cases which seem to occur mostly when the child is from 9 months to 18 months old and the disease seems to be due to a violent fall. This disease is indeed a cruel one for it frequently takes away the use of a hand or arm or sometimes the use of both legs or, sadder still, it sometimes cripples the body and makes the mind defective as well.

The other cases we deal with are more hopeful: I mean the knock kneed, bow legged or crooked limbs. These can in most cases be cured by operations or the wearing of irons for a time.

Now let us consider what is the mission of the ((Cripples)) Union to these children.

In the first place it recognises that crippled children have not the same chances of recreation as able bodied children. And, as recreation is quite as necessary, if not more necessary, in their cure than in other children, for they are apt to brood over their disabilities, the Union then should endeavour to provide a party for them every month during the winter and at least two during the summer months.

Secondly we must recognise that the great majority are delicate and need nourishing food, constant medical advice and most of them need at least 3 weeks in the country every year. Many of them need instruments ((splints etc)): this the Union should see to.

Then again, of these children who are thrown on themselves so much, education is a most important matter and some of them are unable to attend school at all, This matter of education is one of the most important thing for the Union to concern itself with.

Lastly, all of them are handicapped in the attempt to earn a living and the Union must see what can be done to find employment for them and must endeavour to teach them light suitable trades.

It is obvious that this cannot be done by one man or two and so we have to invite the help of lady visitors and parents…"

This is the whole text, with minimal changes and editions of punctuation. Some part of the manuscript is missing at the end but it looks as though he has almost finished.

The strength and urgency of the feelings is striking. The writing is spare and stark: by comparison, the texts of the other addresses, though full of feeling, are measured and not without a degree of elegance. In "Crippled Bairns" he makes no attempt to set the problem in a context of religious belief, there is no biblical text and no reference to Christian, or even moral, values, there are no diversions into allegory. The appeal to the audience is direct – "here is a tragedy: we must act now".

In the manuscript the urgency is even more marked. The handwriting is larger than normal, punctuation is sparse and seems almost randomly distributed, there are many crossings out, insertions, underlinings and uses of abbreviations.

In his book "Years of Caring", a history of the Royal Orthopaedic Hospital, Birmingham, Maurice White records that the Birmingham and District Crippled Children's Union was founded within the Hurst Street Mission in 1896, before Frank's arrival as Assistant Missionary. Its first Secretary was W J Clarke.

The Union seems to have consisted at first of a small group of members of the Mission, mostly women, who visited all the crippled children known to them, about 80 of them at the time, raised funds and did what they could to improve the children's lives.

Frank threw himself wholeheartedly into this work, visiting all the children on the Union's register, building up the group of supporters – donors who gave in cash or kind, including the invaluable hospital or dispensary "notes", visitors who went to see and offer support to the children and their families and people who helped with organisation and fund raising.

He was, no doubt, now doing what he felt most called to do but his 28th year, which also turned out to be his last year with the Mission, brought him personal sadness: his mother died, at the age of 53, on 24 October 1898 and his grandfather Solomon, aged 82, on 20 September 1899. He noted both of these events in his Chronology – the only family deaths recorded there – so they must have affected him greatly.

His mother, Lucy, had had a difficult life in the twenty years since his father's death but had managed to bring up four children, one with a severe disability. Frank's own long search for something he could bring himself to do with his life must have added to her burdens, a fact that he would have recognised. Neither of his sisters had married, nor would they do so. Only his brother Arthur, who described himself as a "fender manufacturer" in the 1901 Census and was then living in Birmingham, seems to have settled down reasonably conventionally.

James Vose Solomon, Lucy's father, was a successful surgeon who had lived to a great age so Frank would not have felt the sense of untimely loss that his mother's death would undoubtedly have occasioned. Nevertheless, the family had depended heavily on Lucy's parents after Daniel died and his grandfather must have been, in some sense, a surrogate father. His death, so soon after Lucy's, must have been a heavy blow.

But these losses do not seem to have affected Frank's interest in the crippled children. The work of the Union went on at an increasing pace, taking more and more of his time until it was decided, probably by the governing body of the Mission, that the Union must go its own way.

An inaugural meeting for a separate Crippled Children's Union was held at Hurst Street on 23 March 1899. Mr Clarke pointed to the growth of the work within the Mission and gave his view that it would be better able to provide the sympathy and help needed by the children if it were to become a separate institution.

It would be hard, especially in the light of subsequent events, to quarrel with this view.

It is not obvious that it was the governing body's wish or intention at this point that Frank should give up his job at the Mission to lead the newly independent Union but before long a decision was made and Frank received the following letter, dated 19 July 1899, from W H Ryland, Secretary of the Mission:

"Dear Mr Mathews

It is my duty to hand to you the following resolution, passed unanimously at the Mission Committee held last evening – "That the Committee recognises the ability and enthusiasm displayed by Mr Mathews, especially in his work among the cripples and other children, but regrets that, having regard to the financial position of the Mission, and the fact that the recently formed Crippled Children's Union will leave him little time to attend to the ordinary work of the Mission, they are unable to renew his engagement as Assistant Missionary, which terminates in September next."

I cannot allow your engagement to terminate without expressing, on my own behalf, my appreciation of your unselfish devotion to you work among the poor children of the town and of the mingled kindness and firmness displayed by you in your work among them, and my hope that you will soon obtain congenial employment in a similar sphere of usefulness."

Mr Ryland's view of the value of the work of the Crippled Children's Union is not in doubt – he served on its committee for several years – but there is something of a mystery in the letter. It puts the decision not to renew Frank's engagement down to a combination of the financial situation of the Mission and pressure from the governing committee for more attention to be paid to its ordinary work, whatever that might have been. Mr Ryland implies that he does not know that Frank has another job waiting for him.

It may possibly be that the elders of the mission thought that the political content of Frank's addresses was not appropriate, though any offence is likely to have been mild. It also does seem entirely possible in view of Frank's relations with committees in general later in life that there were some who felt things might be more comfortable with a less turbulent priest.

Whether or not this was so Frank was out of the one job and no doubt delighted to take on the other, the only problem being that he needed a status and some money to live on. A temporary arrangement was made to support Frank, after a fashion, in his new job and he was appointed Superintendent of the Union on 25 September 1899 at a much reduced salary of £59 p.a. for six months. He became Secretary in July 1900 on the retirement of Mr Clarke.

1899 – 1909 THE CRIPPLES UNION

At the turn of the century Birmingham was a fairly compact town of around half a million people, the fourth largest population in England. It was increasing by around 5,000 per year, more than accounted for by the excess of births over deaths. Later, it would also increase in size by taking in already populated areas round about.

Although poor people depended on charity for anything beyond the rudimentary medical help they could afford to pay for, there was beginning to be an effective public health system. The death rate decreased dramatically from 19.9 per thousand in 1895 to 16.1 per thousand in 1905, because of the success of public health measures.

The authorities were concentrating, rightly, on acute infectious diseases some of which, scarlet fever, for example, occurred as periodic epidemics. They were well aware that these diseases were most common under the poor and overcrowded conditions in what the Medical Officer of Health called the less sanitary parts of the City and did what they could in the short term to improve the state of affairs. In 1899, for example, the Health Visitors visited 11,700 houses and, as a result, issued 1,800 notices to landlords to undertake sanitary work. Three years later an increased number of Visitors made 32,000 primary visits and 10,100 return visits discovering in the process 8,800 households that had illnesses of one sort or another within them.

The eventual solution to these problems came over the next fifty years from slum clearance, the improvement of the water supply, the discovery of antibiotics, the National Health Service and increased general prosperity. In the short term the authorities could only work to inhibit the spread of disease by programmes of inoculation and by such measures as disinfection of properties where infectious disease was discovered.

Almost ten percent of deaths in the years 1894 – 1898 were ascribed to tubercular diseases, about 950 per year. About 850 of these were from consumption of the lungs (phthisis). Thus, although the figures varied a little from year to year, deaths caused directly by tubercular bone disease were not considered significant enough to be reported separately as a public health issue. Its crippling effects, which were to be the focus of Frank's work, were, as he later made clear, also greatly under reported.

The fourth annual report of The Crippled Children's Union (1902 – 03) starts with a statistical summary of cases on the register and recalls that, at the time when the Union became independent, there were 330 names on the register and that is was expected, following estimates made in London, that about 200 remained to be discovered. By the date of the report there were 740 names and "unhappily there ((was)) no reason to suppose that our aim to get in touch with every crippled child of the poor ((was)) as yet anything like realised". 338 new cases had been identified during the year. Over 200 new cases were discovered each year for several years to come and, though many stayed on the register only temporarily the number of children cared for each year hovered around 1000 for the next decade.

This recruitment rate represents between one and two percent of the child population of Birmingham at the time, and would have meant that, in the poorer areas especially, crippled children were a common sight on the streets where, indeed, many of them had to try to earn some sort of contribution of their families' incomes.

The most common afflictions, all of which are now rare in Britain, were paralysis – 86 of the 338 new cases – spinal disease – 73 – hip disease – 49 – knee joint disease – 21 (all forms of tubercular bone disease) and rickets – 15. Frank and his co-workers set themselves to doing something for the sufferers in the appalling conditions of the time.

Many people were aware of the problem. The largest number of the Union's new cases – 105 – were referred by School Board officials, who had no public agency to turn to. 44 came from parents of children already under the care of the Union, 40 from the hospitals, 27 from Lady Health Visitors and 20 from the Union's own visitors. Frank found 19 himself.

To do something effective to help even a modest proportion of all the sufferers that were being discovered Frank had first of all to set up an organisation that would convince potential donors that the Union would be a worthy recipient of their money. He needed to show not only that there was a heartrending need for something to be done, but that he could be trusted to use their money effectively and account for it properly. Although he already had a good record he was not yet a significant public figure so he had to show that there were a sufficient number of people that the public would trust who would, in turn, trust him.

He set about this by persuading leading citizens to express their support by accepting office in the organisation of the Union. An early list starts with an impressive list of patrons beginning with the Lord Mayor of Birmingham as President, fifteen Vice-Presidents – the Countess of Warwick, Lord Calthorp, the Lord Bishop of Coventry, five Members of parliament, led by Joseph Chamberlain, businessmen, including George Cadbury and Edward Ansell, the brewer, both of who would be consistent supporters, and other worthies.

The Hon. Treasurer, Hon Secretary and Secretary (Frank Mathews) are followed by a Council of 18, including Arthur Holden, a Committee of 18 and three Hon. Surgeons all of whom were, or would become, surgeons to the Royal Orthopaedic Hospital.

Frank would stay with the Crippled Children's Union, later the Birmingham Cripples' Union, until March 1922. In July 1900 he was made Secretary, a post he held for the remainder of his time.

In his twenty three years he combined prodigious feats of organisation with an enormous amount of personal intervention in the lives of the suffering. The methods that were deployed, and the means for deploying them, developed in many ways over the years but the general principles underlying the development emerged quite early in the Union's history.

The position after only a few years' work is described in the fourth Annual Report. This report is much fuller and is written with greater passion than its immediate successors and the style of the writing suggests that it was mostly written by Frank himself and that it sets out his agenda for the immediate future of the Union.
Already, by this time, the work can be seen to have been developing in three strands.

The first was described as "immediate relief" which was offered to all newly identified sufferers. Of the 338 new cases 197 are described as "Visited and advised only" but the report explains that

> "That must not be understood as meaning that visitation and advice was all that was wanted……It was all that under the circumstances the Union could do for them…..Nor does it mean that should acuter need arise they will (not) certainly receive…further help. They will if funds are sufficient, if, in other words, it lies in our power to send them to a Nursing or Convalescent Home in the country. We are in the same trying position in regards to hundreds of other cases".

And later:

> "If in many instances we are not in a position to do all that is necessary, we may at least claim that we do alleviate the sufferings in even the worst cases. No child known to us goes without such immediate relief as it lies in our power to render. We can at least lend a water pillow, a bath chair or spinal carriage, supply nourishments, secure the attendance of a district nurse, send a visitor, or it may be obtain admission to the special school….The visitation is a matter of great importance. If the child is seen by no one else it is at least visited regularly by Mr Mathews, who puts himself into close personal touch with every case and is thoroughly acquainted with it. There is also splendid work to be done by volunteers, who in addition to a warm heart have plenty of common sense. And we want more of them. There must be

hundreds of ladies in Birmingham who would be glad to help if they only knew how fine is the use to which they can put a few hours every week".

The second, curative, strand started with helping children to gain access to medical or surgical care, usually through the provision of hospital notes. The report says that "506 cases have been under treatment at the Hospitals and Medical Charities. 1057 Notes for Hospitals and Convalescent Homes have been received in response to appeals"

Before the days of the National Health Service many hospitals and other medical facilities were charities supported largely by local patrons. In return for their subscriptions patrons would receive each year a number of "Notes" each entitling the bearer to consultation, treatment or medicines. These notes were, in a sense, a kind of currency and, like cash, they could be donated to charities such as the Union that would put them to good use.

The Notes received by the Union were used to obtain "instruments" – leg braces, surgical boots and so forth - to procure consultations and hospital admissions in urgent cases and to pay for stays at convalescent homes.

In his work for the Cinderella Club Frank had been struck by the way in which children who lived in the dreadful conditions of the Birmingham slums were helped by even quite short stays in peaceful surroundings. It is clear that he very soon became convinced that crippled children could be helped by similar treatment and even after only three years the Union was investing a great part of its effort into convalescence. The idea that quite difficult and complex medical conditions could be helped by a period of comfortable normality was one that guided much of his subsequent work.

There was a great shortage of convalescent facilities, it being said that only about 80 beds suitable for crippled children were to be found in the area around Birmingham. So, as early as the second year of the Union's existence the Union had invested £50 to open its own cottage convalescent home at Chadwick End near Knowle, a few miles southeast of the City. The cottage home had a matron and an assistant matron and could take six children in winter and ten in summer. It was to continue in use for ten years.

In those first years 245 children were sent away for convalescence, 80 of them to Chadwick End and the remainder to more than a dozen other places, almost all in Birmingham or the country immediately around.

The third strand was to do with education and employment. Many of the children on the Union's register could barely leave their homes, let alone survive the rigours of ordinary elementary (primary) schools. Even if they did manage to obtain some education it was very difficult for them to find work to support themselves – no disability rights then. Frank and the Union set vigorously about solving these problems.

One of the early successes of the Union, related in its fourth report, was in persuading the Birmingham School Board to open a Special School for crippled children (itself a pioneering venture) in Dean Street, near the Bull Ring in the old centre of the city. The fourth Report goes at length into the school's earliest experiences:

> "….the unqualified success of the Special School, which owes its origin to our initiative. There are now 43 children in attendance, very nearly as many as the Dean Street room has accommodation for. The late School Board made an ideal selection when they appointed Miss Bennett as head mistress. In her, her assistant, Miss Norton, and the two nurses, the children have, and know they have, real friends whose whole soul is in their work. It is safe to say that in spite of all the disabilities under which these children suffer there is no happier or more interested school in the city."

It quotes Miss Bennett…

> "On September 1st 1902, the late School Board laid the foundation to a work which has long been needed in our city. A School for Crippled Children was opened in the St. Martin's

Mission Hall, Dean Street, and a new life was opened out for these children, who had hitherto been debarred from the benefits of the schoolroom.

The selection of the children depends upon their physical condition. Those who are unfit to attend ordinary schools and are not sufficiently ill to be in hospital, may, after passing a medical examination by Dr. Simon, now have instruction and guidance from their teachers, care and supervision of their physical comfort from their nurses, and companionship and amusement from their fellow scholars at Dean Street. One of the happiest hours of the day is the 'dinner hour' when every child has a hot dinner of meat, vegetables and pudding, provided by the Cripples Union….."

The Report goes on:

"An unusual feature of this school is that the children strongly object to the holidays. One was recently heard to say that he didn't mean to break up. A note on his case soon reveals the reason. He is hopelessly crippled, although nine months' stay in the country cured him of the active disease. His father is epileptic, and he has a stepmother. Naturally he is a good deal of trouble, and apparently during the holidays he would be put to bed and left there, unable to help himself. Not much wonder that holidays, to him, are a tiresome and unreasonable arrangement….

…It seems a great pity that the Board of Education will not permit the entrance of a child before it is seven, and insists on its leaving at sixteen (normal compulsory schooling was from five to fourteen). On the one hand it may be pointed out that for children in normal health under that age there are infant schools. There can be no reason for depriving the cripples who are too delicate to enter them of this advantage, except the difficulty of making special provision…..With regard to the superior limit. We get cripples who are fourteen or fifteen when they enter the school, having received no previous education, and it seems hard that they should have so restricted a chance. The one or two years cannot be of any great value. It is no easy matter for a girl or boy of that age to start learning. If it could be arranged to continue the course in such special cases a real boon would be conferred."

Much of the Union's effort was devoted to helping sufferers after they had completed whatever education they could get. Many areas of work were barred to them because of their lack of physical strength but it was clearly seen that they could not be abandoned without some means of earning a living, or at least contributing to their own upkeep.

> "We have been somewhat keenly disappointed to find that manufacturers have not responded to our appeals to give employment to boys quite able for it. During three years we have obtained situations for eight. All are in the place they went to, and giving, we understand, every satisfaction. And that, we are convinced, would be the common experience"

This was the experience of the Union with the response from the world at large. It decided to take on the problem itself.

> "A very useful industry from which in the two previous years we derived a considerable sum is paper flower making….But one thing has now definitely impressed itself upon us. For paper flowers there is only a philanthropic sale. Their manufacture is not a stable industry., which can be securely relied upon….Whenever possible we are convinced that the children should be assisted to find work which offers more certain prospects".

> "….we feel that we have reason for gratification…that during the past year an important industry has been started for the girls. After much consideration, it was found that hand-loom weaving combined the advantage of light, interesting and educative employment with a fair prospect of affording a means of livelihood….. A legacy of £250 enabled the committee to start work in September last. A light airy house (No. 320 Summer Lane) was taken, a competent teacher engaged, and several looms imported from Norway. Although the school is still in its infancy, much good work has already been produced …The prices are moderate and are fixed on a strictly commercial basis…"

> "Dr Lawrie very kindly visited the school, and reported most favourably upon the suitability of the work for cripples,

particularly for cases of spinal deformity, and the health of the girls bears out his opinion...."

"We are most anxious to get an industry, such as Surgical Boot-making started for boys. The only thing which causes us to hesitate is the lack of means."

The weaving school eventually separated from the Union and continued as a separate Society. It was not, in the end found possible to establish a boot manufactory.

But to return to the fourth report, Franks greatest ambition, even at this early stage in the Union's development, is set out in an appeal for funds for a Nursing or Convalescent Home to permit the accommodation of many more children for breaks of a few weeks and with a capacity great enough to permit stays of the two years that he believes to be necessary for the cure of the worst cases. He estimates the cost at £10,000 to purchase land, build a home and provide an endowment of £300 per year.

Also in the report he welcomes the formation of a Roman Catholic branch of the Union and the arrival in Birmingham of the "Guild of Brave Poor Things" " a society which in other towns, and especially in London, has done splendid service. Its object is to come to the aid, in every way at once wise and possible, of persons over fourteen years of age who are crippled. It thus steps in at the point where we are compelled, as a general rule, to stop and should prove a valuable adjunct to our work. Already we have handed over to its committee 34 cases...." The two bodies were to amalgamate later to form the Birmingham Cripples Union.

As was always Frank's custom details are given of a few cases for which help is asked and there is a report on the cases for which help was asked in the last report. Two of the former were:

"W. W. suffers from spinal disease, is one of a large family, and lives in a very unhealthy part of the town. He has been ordered 18 months at the seaside, and this, it is hoped, will quite cure him. The cost is 7s per week, towards which his parents pay 1/6, as much as they can possibly afford."

and;

"L. L. A very sad case. The child suffers from spinal disease and has a diseased elbow. Her mother is dying of spinal disease. There are three other children and a stepfather who drinks. The child herself will die unless removed from home to the country immediately. Will not someone give us the 6s. per week required?"

and of the follow up, he reports;

"F. B. and M. L. we were enabled to send into the country for a year, by the proceeds of a Jumble Sale arranged by the Misses Mathews (Frank's sisters). The treatment has worked wonders in the case of F. B. M. L. unhappily proved to be incurable, and has been handed over to the Guild of Brave Poor Things, having passed the limit of age below which we have to confine our work."

A sad reminder that treatment was not always successful though the other half dozen cases reported on all show at least some positive results.

Frank was a resourceful and inventive fund raiser: part of his success came from the care he always took care to acknowledge publicly every donation of cash or kind and every subscription. Half of the fourth report, 19 pages, is given over to acknowledgements of sums of money ranging from 1s to £71/1/8d and items ranging from cooking utensils for the school to seeds for the cottage garden, toys and a pair of crutches.

The income to the general fund in that fourth year, ending 31 March 1903, was about £950. Translation into modern terms is difficult because both expectations and relative costs have changed but, for example, this amount of money would have bought a block of four good small houses in the new Bournville estate or would have kept ten working class families out of poverty for a year. Obviously, from what was done with it, it was a substantial amount of money.

Money was raised by a variety of means. £250 came from subscriptions – money given regularly year upon year - £300 from general donations and £150 from donations for specific objects. £77 came from a total of 90 collecting cards and boxes and occasional collections, all individually recorded. Other receipts included money from the sale of children's work, £49, parents' payments, £28, and dinner payments, £29.

The list of donors and subscribers has over 650 entries, mostly naming individuals but also including associations such as the Acorn Club, which made the biggest single donation of the year, the proceeds of a concert, £8/9/5, sent by Miss L Bosworth, four members of the Hurst Street cycling club, 5/-, and the girls of King Edwards School, Bath Row, £13.

The individuals included many who were prominent in the life of the City; Edward Ansell, seven members of the Cadbury family, Joseph Chamberlain, Sir Oliver Lodge, as well as Frank's grandmother and his two sisters.

Separate accounts include an "Industry Account" whose principal receipt is £26/3/11 from the sale of weaving work, the Christmas Tree fund, £40/2/10 collected by the Misses Mathews and the Misses Jones and the "Jumble sale organised by the Misses Mathews", £18/8/6 collected by them in donations and £7/11/3, after expenses, from the sale itself.

The report concludes, fittingly enough, with a printed "Form of Legacy" and a blank Banker's Order form, both in favour of the Union.

The next four years, possibly the most enjoyable for Frank, saw steady progress. The number of children on the register increased steadily to 827 with further 73 and 52 in branches at Smethwick and Selly Oak and about 70 in the Roman Catholic branch. Income to the general fund of the main Union had doubled by 1906. Legacies and donations to the building fund for the wished for nursing home had brought the total accumulated to almost £2,000 of the £10,000 originally thought to be needed.

There is continuing reference to the difficulty of finding employment for boys, offset by stories of successful placements. A small number of girls were being taught shorthand and typing.

The report for 1903 - 4 refers to the start of a home working industry for children too crippled to work away from home. The newly appointed teacher, Miss Wynn Thomas, visited the children in their homes to teach crafts such as basket making and, very soon, money was being raised from the sale of work. The enterprise prospered and two years later skilled workers were being paid 6 – 7s per week and there was an advertisement for the wares in the Annual Report of the Union.

In 1904 it was also reported that, eighteen months from its start, the Special Council School had 65 pupils with another 30 – 40 on the waiting list, a branch being opened at Jenkin Street a year later. The School was to move to George Street West in 1907.

Other activities included an annual Christmas party in the Town Hall, donated by Edward Ansell, an annual summer outing and picnic at the Manor House in Northfield, home of George and Elizabeth Cadbury, a car outing provided by members of the Midland Motor Union, and the establishment of three new play hours in different parts of the city.

A Workmans' Auxiliary Committee was set up in September 1905 after a meeting at Frank's house, to raise funds, largely through appeals to working people. Maurice White gives an account of the tireless activities of its Hon. Secretary for almost 50 years, A E Wort, himself crippled in childhood by a fall.

1907 – 9 saw a number of important developments including the amalgamation of the industrial work of the Union and that of the Adult Cripples' Guild (whose former title had perhaps been found too patronising) under the direction of Miss Thomas. This arrangement, which included the appointment of a part time assistant, was seen as a step toward the integration of the two societies brought about two years later, Frank remaining de facto leader of the new organisation. The home manufactory continued to prosper, as did the weaving school.

It will be recalled that from the earliest days of the Union home visiting of children and their families had been regarded as "a matter of great importance" as part of the "immediate relief which was offered to all newly identified sufferers" and that: "If the child is seen by no one else it is at least visited regularly by Mr Mathews, who puts himself into close personal touch with every case and is thoroughly acquainted with it."

Five years later it is noted in the 1907 – 8 Report that Frank was visiting each child on the books three times per year but that even this prodigious effort, together with that of volunteer visitors, was not sufficient to provide the level of support that was felt to be needed. Consequently, three assistants were being trained, the training including a two months' course in nursing, bandaging and splint measurement as well as instruction in massage.

The next year it was reported that 7,000 to 8,000 home visits were being made during the year, two to each home by Frank and five by the assistants and that

> "each time careful notes are made, advice given, notice taken whether previous suggestions have been carried out. ((Frank did not shrink from using legal sanctions when he detected wilful neglect.)) Not only does the crippled child benefit from these visits, but other members of the household also. The mere fact that there is a crippled child in the family usually means that one or both of the parents are delicate, and several of the other children. These latter are carefully supervised (if necessary sent to hospital), and there is no doubt that we are able to save many from being entered on our register as cripples. Thus we are doing preventive as well as curative work."

But the most significant happening of the two years was the announcement and follow up of the news that George Cadbury had bought The Woodlands, a large house standing in nearly five acres of ground, and presented it to the Union to be used as a Nursing and Convalescent Home capable, it was thought, of accommodating 60 – 70 children.

Thus, Frank was on the way to getting his dearest wish. There was much to do to complete the conversion and much money still to find but The Woodlands did open, ushering in a new, and quite different, phase in the life of the Union, changing Frank's life, in the process, in ways that he did not always find comfortable.

BOURNVILLE

On 29th May 1901 Frank received a letter from Evelyn Holden at his home address in Summer Road, Edgbaston. Only the envelope has survived but it seems a fair bet that the content was of a social nature.

Evelyn, who was born in Moseley on the southern outskirts of Birmingham in 1877, was the youngest of Arthur and Emma Holden's seven children. She had four sisters, Effie, born in 1867, Winifred, born in 1869, Edith, 1871, and Violet, 1873. Her two brothers were Arthur Kenneth, 1870 and Charles Bernard, 1875.

She was brought up in very comfortable middle class circumstances. Her parents moved house several times but always lived in rural or semi rural surroundings. Arthur Holden and Evelyn's brother Bernard worked in the business near to the centre of Birmingham and Arthur, at least, spent much of his time, outside working hours in the city, in his many public activities.

When she was in her twenties Evelyn also spent much of her time in the centre of Birmingham. Like her sisters Edith and Violet, she went to the Birmingham Municipal School of Art, then widely regarded as the best of the provincial art colleges. She was probably the most talented of the three and won prizes – one of the books of her edition of Stevenson has a prize bookplate from the School - and scholarships for free tuition. She joined her sisters in book illustration and saw several of her works in print. There is no doubt that her work was extremely competent. It seems to have been commercially interesting as well and it seems likely that she could have made a good career in illustration.

Frank was a frequent visitor to the Holdens' home and Evelyn and her sisters took an interest in Frank's work with children, first through the Cinderella Club, which their father supported by the loan of his cottage, and then through the Hurst Street Mission and the Crippled Children's Union. The interest developed for Frank and Evelyn into friendship and love. On October 13th 1902 they became formally engaged. He was thirty one years old, she was twenty five.

Their wish to marry was not, at first, greeted with enthusiasm by Evelyn's family. Frank, though obviously socially acceptable, was, by the Holdens' standards poor and without prospects. But this was not the problem. Arthur Holden's record as an employer, as a public servant, as a philanthropist and as a supporter of Frank's endeavours demonstrates clearly enough that he approved of Frank's work. He would probably have felt that the family could well afford to support the couple financially as part of his contribution to the well being of the needy – as, in large measure it subsequently did.

Their concern was for Evelyn's health. She had been delicate as a child and they believed that her delicacy was an inevitable complement of her artistic talent. They believed that Frank's extraordinary commitment to his work would not leave him able to give her the special care she needed.

Apparently this concern was not shared by all her family. Edith was very matter of fact about the supposed perils of minor physical hardship. But Evelyn's mother wrote to Frank stressing Evelyn's unusual sensitivity and the care she needed in both body and spirit. In her biography of Edith, Ina Taylor quotes her as writing:

"You are very similar and you both want to live a simple outward life of help to others and trust in one another, and really you should be very happy." She asked Frank not to allow Evelyn to become a vegetarian like himself because "you will not have her long."

The couple were married on April 30th 1904 at Newhall Hill Chapel in Birmingham. The ceremony was kept simple, perhaps because of Evelyn's mother's failing health. Evelyn's youngest sister Violet was her bridesmaid and her brother Bernard acted as groom. They were married for forty four years and Evelyn survived into her nineties. She did become a vegetarian, though fish and the breast of chicken were permitted.

After her marriage Evelyn continued to take an interest in drawing and painting. She owned a good number of books about the old masters and the artists of her time and she occasionally produced drawings herself. But, unlike Edith, who drew and painted professionally all her life and became famous many years later for the "Country Diary of an Edwardian Lady", she seems to have abandoned any idea of making a career as an artist in favour of support for Frank's work

* * *

The couple had to find somewhere to live. George Cadbury and several other members of the Cadbury family had been among the earliest subscribers to the Crippled Children's Union and Frank would have known about the Model Village of Bournville that was just beginning to take shape. It would have had an obvious appeal to him.

Shortly before his marriage Frank received a letter from J H Barlow, Secretary of the Bournville Village Trust, addressed to him at the offices of the Cripples Union:

"Dear Sir

In reply to your letter of yesterday I think we could probably arrange to let you have one of the new houses in Maple Road if it would meet your requirements. The rents will probably be 9/6 for the smaller houses and 10/6 for the larger ones but these figures are not finally settled. As we are receiving a large number of applications for these houses I shall be glad to hear from you at an early date whether you wish to have one."

Frank noted, on the letter, "accepted at 10/6".

The history of Bournville and the activities of the Bournville Village Trust are described comprehensively in Michael Harrison's "Bournville

– Model Village to Garden Suburb". The Trust Deed sets out the primary object as:

> "…the amelioration of the condition of the working classes and the labouring population in and around Birmingham, and elsewhere in Great Britain, by the provision of improved dwellings, with gardens and open spaces to be enjoyed therewith, and by giving them facilities…for purchasing and acquiring the necessities of life."

Although the Trust was registered as a charity it was never intended as a source of hand outs:

> "The Founder…desires that the rent of such dwellings may if practicable be fixed on such a basis as to make them accessible to persons of the labouring and working classes, whom it is his desire to attract from the crowded and insanitary tenements which they now inhabit, without ever placing them in the position of being recipients of a bounty."

Neither was it meant to be either a company village – the proportion of houses occupied by Cadbury workers never exceeded fifty percent – or a one class district. There were few rich people, the Cadbury family and a few of their senior staff occupied large houses within the Bournville area, but it was the Trust's policy from the start to attract a proportion of middle class residents.

Thus, although George Cadbury knew of Frank's work and supported the Cripples Union there is no reason to suppose that the offer of a house came as a result of his influence, or even that he knew about it. Barlow may have known about Frank's work but, whether he did or not, he would have thought that the Mathews fitted perfectly into the range of people that it was the policy of the Trust to attract.

The original main purpose of the Trust was "to provide healthy dwellings for people with plenty of air and space" and it concentrated its effort at first on creating a model village in the area immediately to the North of the Bournville works which had been started in 1879 on a site on the edge of Birmingham.

Maple Road was one of the first roads to be built up after the formation of the Bournville Village Trust in 1900: by 1906 most, or all, of its building plots had been filled. It is quite likely that number 47, which the Mathews lived in for all their married lives and which Evelyn continued to occupy until her death, was ready for them almost exactly at the date of their marriage.

Their house is no more than a hundred yards from The Green where there were a few shops – H W Smith, who sold grocery and dairy products, James Healy, bootmaker and repairer, W Sanders, confectioner and Alfred Allely ironmonger. The Green would soon be surrounded by public buildings - the Friends Meeting House, infant and junior schools, the latter's square tower now carrying a famous carillon of bells, the Church Hall and the Ruskin Hall School of Arts and Crafts.

Like most of the houses in Maple Road, number 47 was one of a semi detached pair. It had a good sized garden, the Trust's policy at that time being that no house might cover more than a quarter of its building plot and that housing density should not exceed six per acre. It was not large, having a sitting room, dining room, kitchen and entrance hall downstairs, but was by no means the smallest on the estate. The earliest workmen's cottages would have had just a living room and a good sized kitchen downstairs and would have been let at 6/- to 7/-.

All the houses in Maple Road were in the Western side with sunny back gardens backing on to those of houses in the parallel Linden Road, the main route through Bournville and later part of Birmingham's outer ring road. On the other side of Maple Road was Camp Wood, an old woodland said to have Civil War associations which was retained when the estate was laid out. Two medieval timber framed buildings, Selly Manor and Minworth Greaves, were moved from elsewhere and re-erected on the Southern corner plot almost opposite number 47. Myra Wynn Thomas was a neighbour of the Mathews up a gentle hill at number 7.

The Mathews duly moved in after their marriage taking with them, in response to the family's concerns, Rosanna, Evelyn's former nanny. Its seems that, at first, Evelyn's health was not particularly good and Rosanna may well have been needed. In fact, the Mathews had some domestic help throughout their tenure of number 47 so despite the modesty of their accommodation, to say nothing of the shortness of money that they often experienced, they retained some semblance of the middle class lifestyle to which they had been brought up.

For aesthetic reasons the Mathews furnished their house simply. The front room was often used for work for Frank's charities. It contained a table, several old but restored windsor chairs, including two fine carvers, and a large wooden dresser, the lower part of which was old, the shelves above having been an early 20th century replacement, presumably, for an earlier set. The dresser was ornamented with a collection of, mostly modern, Staffordshire blue china. The couple used the back room as their principal living room. In addition to alcove bookshelves it had two armchairs and a beige carpet. Their bedroom contained two plain iron framed single beds, rather far apart and each with its own enamelled chamber pot. The restored items were bought early in their marriage from a dealer near the Bull Ring, in the centre of Birmingham, who specialised in supplying such things to people like the Mathews who wanted simple good looking furniture of a general William Morris tendency but who couldn't afford to pay much for it.

Gardening was high on the list of George Cadbury's priorities for Bournville. He had greatly enjoyed the gardens of the houses that he had lived in and he believed that gardening was the best leisure occupation for a working man since it combined healthy exercise with an opportunity to be in touch with nature. It had the added advantages of being an alternative to the public house – often the only spare time option for inner city men – and of being a source of food. The sale of alcoholic drinks was not allowed on the estate though there was, from 1900, a Temperance Tavern, the Old Farm Inn, which sold food and non alcoholic drinks including, of course, drinking chocolate.

Garden sizes were set, in the early Bournville, at the maximum that it was thought that a healthy man could cultivate with a spade in his spare time and it was calculated that a garden could produce about 2/6 worth of food per week, more than making up the difference between Bournville and inner city rents. The gardens of new houses were laid out by the Trust's gardeners before they were handed to tenants who were also able to call on the gardening department for advice if they thought they needed it. The initial laying out also included the provision of fruit trees that were kept pruned for the first three years – this provision continued until at least the 1960s.

There was every indication that the tenants as a whole agreed enthusiastically with George Cadbury's views. Gardens were almost all kept to a high standard, with flowers in the front and near the back of the house and fruit and vegetables further away, and there were annual gardening competitions. The houses were usually designed with the kitchen overlooking the garden so that the housewife going about her work there would be in touch with nature.

Frank's earlier experiences had left him with a lifelong love of gardening though whether he ever grew vegetables is not known. Later in his life the back garden, which was about 50 yards deep and twelve wide, was laid out as a series of herbaceous borders one behind the other with a path threading its way between. In the borders he grew a fine collection of hardy perennials including phlox, helenium, and many varieties of michaelmas daisies.

* * *

Frank's maternal grandmother, Mary Welch Solomon died, aged ninety, in the early part of 1905. She had been a subscriber to the Cripples Union and a last donation in memoriam is recorded in the report for that year. His two aunts Sophia and Charlotte continued to subscribe as did his sisters, correctly identified in the Union's reports as Miss Mathews and Miss E Mathews.

By this time Frank would have come into his inheritance from his grandfather. He was to have roughly one fifteenth of the estate. This amounted to a few hundred pounds, enough to buy a decent house, if he had a mind, which, apparently he didn't since he lived the remainder of his life in a rented property, or to provide him with an income that would more or less cover the rent.

At about this time, and, perhaps, using her inheritance, Frank's sister Ethel bought two small cottages at Llwyngwril, a village just South of Barmouth on the West coast of Wales. One was to live in, one was to let to holiday makers. This was in an area that Frank already knew well from his many holidays in the area: it was to be an important centre for the Mathews for many years.

Frank visited Ethel regularly for the remainder of her life - she died in 1944 - staying, at least in later years, as a lodger in one or other of the larger houses in the village. It seems that, at first, Evelyn did not go to Llwyngwryl with Frank, or, at least, not always, for a small collection of picture postcards written to her from Wales has survived. There are thirteen of them, dated between July 1906 and August 1910, and sent to Evelyn either at Maple Road or at Gowan Bank, Olton, Near Birmingham, her father's house. Six were postmarked at Llwyngwryl, the remainder at places nearby.

The first, postmarked Bala, July 1st 1906 reads "Just to let you know I have had a delightful day and am really feel((ing)) better. Will send a letter tomorrow shall not have time tonight." The letter, sadly, has not been preserved: perhaps the postcard owes its survival to its greatly faded picture of Bala lake.

The next three come from a holiday in 1908. On the fifth of August he writes "No news today and I am going out for the day so am just sending you my love. It is a cool grey day, dry with a high wind and drifts of showers. Thanks for all your nice letters. Lots of love." The second, which has a nice photograph of Arthog on the Mawddach estuary, becomes illegible at the point where it might otherwise be possible to understand what it is about and the third, dated the fourteenth, which simply says "arrive Snow Hill ((Birmingham)) 7.50" is mainly of interest because it also carries a brief note from Ethel apologising for not having had the time to write and thanking Evelyn for biscuits. It is interesting because it makes it possible to identify Ethel's characteristic and beautiful handwriting when it occurs elsewhere.

Frank went to Llwyngwryl twice in 1909, the first time for a few days in June. He tells of a glorious day which has left him "wonderfully refreshed", promises a letter "tomorrow" and send his love to "Pa", presumably Arthur Holden. The second time he stayed for longer while Evelyn went to Gowan Bank. On August 1st he wrote; "Its raining, its rained all day. Still we are cheerful. Ethel really is getting on very well. Jack (Ramsden) comes on Tuesday so there will be sunshine whether it rains or not." And, two days later; "had another really gorgeous day on Cader. Feel ever so much better."

On the 7th; "We have just been up the river to Penmaen Pool. Took Ethel who enjoyed it immensely. Have had a bath to take the stiffness off! I shall write you a letter tomorrow. It has been so jolly to have Jack here." And, despite his promise, on the next day; "I hoped to write you a letter today but Jack discovered late last night that there was no train and that he had to ride to Corwen to catch one so I have ridden to Bala with him and am just now starting back. ((The card is postmarked Bala, 7.15pm.)) We have had such a good time. I am quite lonely now he has gone. I had to start before I got your letter so can't answer it in full. I will do so. Much love from Frank."

This is the first suggestion that Frank had taken to motor cycling. It is confirmed next year when he writes, on July 27th; "I've had a good day. Cycled over…to Llanbedrog. Am glad you are going to Bourton on the 3rd. I come on 14th. Leave here 13th probably unless you would like me to come earlier. The fog burned off this morning thank goodness." And on August 4th, addressed to "The Horse and Groom, Bourton on the Hill"; "Am having a grand day's motor cycling in Snowdonia enjoying it…write tomorrow."

Although they form only part of one side of a correspondence these brief messages make it perfectly plain that the couple enjoyed a very affectionate relationship. Also, the repeated references to Frank's feeling better for his holidays show how much he relied on the release they provided from the stress of his work. In later life he said that he would find it impossible to continue without at least a weekend away every six weeks.

The references to Ethel suggest long term ill health and, perhaps, give a hint as to why Frank chose to pass many of his holidays in that period at Llwyngwryl. Later, he made a habit of going there at the New Year, probably without Evelyn, and spending his summer holiday camping, with Evelyn, at Cae Du, a tiny site at the seaward end of a steep sided valley on the coast a few miles south of Llwyngwril.

There is no doubt that Frank found his work stressful, perhaps especially in the years after George Cadbury's donation of The Woodlands. This made it possible for him to fulfil he desire for a convalescent home but it also required him to be involved in a great deal more administrative work, something he made no secret of disliking when it involved coping with committees. This is perhaps what made him restless for a while.

In February 1913 he thought seriously of applying to be Secretary of the Bradford Guild of Help and went so far as to obtain four testimonials, from G H Bryson, Chairman of the Cripples Union, W J Clarke, Addison Charlesworth, Unitarian Minister at Highgate and J L Paton, High Master of Manchester Grammar School and President of the Manchester and Salford Crippled Children's Help Society.

All the testimonials praise him without reservation. Mr Bryson adds his best wishes for Frank's future which "is worthy of better recognition than he is now receiving, and though we should be extremely sorry to lose his services, I recognise that he is taking the right course in applying for a position with better prospects." - without explaining why the prospects should be better in Bradford.

Mr Charlesworth, who was involved with the Cripples Union in its earliest days says:

"…The story of the Union is one of continuous progress, and it will be readily admitted by all who have taken part in it that this is mainly due to his personal qualities and work. On this particular branch of social work I daresay his experience is unrivalled in England today. It has brought him into close contact with the lives of the poor, and given him an insight and a power of dealing with the problems affecting them beyond the demands of his specific work…"

Mr Paton's letter is, perhaps the most touching:

"I have known Mr Frank Mathews for some score of years. I know something of his work. I wish I knew more. His work among the cripples of Birmingham and district is a model of what ought to be in all big towns. This work, with its organisation, and all its different ramifications, has been entirely built up by Mr Mathews. This has involved a study of all sorts of questions, medical, industrial, social, municipal. It means the organisation of work done by 'helpers', both honorary, and paid. In all these respects, Mr Mathews has proved his exceptional capacity. The motive power that has been sufficient for all this is love. I do not know anyone who has more of that motive power than he."

Frank kept these testimonials – they all seem to be the originals – and there is no sign that he ever sent in an application for the job. It is hard to believe that his application would have failed, still harder that it would not have been acknowledged, so it seems that he did not apply. He may have felt, on reflection, that he would find the work undertaken by the Guild of Help unsatisfying. Typically, this would have concentrated on visiting the poorest families in the town and advising them how to make the best of their circumstances. It would have been not entirely dissimilar to what the volunteers of the Crippled Children's Union had been doing fifteen or so years before when they had little else to offer but that work had progressed a long way down a path of material intervention. Guild of Help volunteers were strongly discouraged from giving money, though some could not always bear to follow that instruction.

Not applying to Bradford did not put an end to Frank's restlessness, however, for at about the same time he drafted a letter to Mr Bryson. The draft is undated but its content suggests that it was written in 1913. Mr Bryson's resignation as chairman was announced in the report for the year ending March 31st 1913. The draft is in Ethel's handwriting:

"Dear Mr Bryson

At the moment when some reorganisation of the office is under consideration (Christine Cox was appointed joint Secretary in 1914) I shall be glad if the Committee will look at my position in relation to the general future of the Union. I have been secretary for 14 years. During that time the work has grown enormously, and the response of the public to our needs shows that the interest in and appreciation of that work has grown also and is still growing. There is no reason to anticipate that we are yet near the limit.

When I first became Secretary I was paid at the rate of £50 a year. A special appeal was made to enable the payment of a more adequate salary and for four or five years I was paid £100 a year. I was deeply interested in the work, and content to accept what the Union could afford. At present I have £215. But I am married, and I am over forty years of age. It will be obvious that it is necessary and my duty to look to the future.

I am not ambitious, and do not want to make any extravagant request. I recognise that work for charity can never be paid on a high scale. I am content that this should be so for, as I hope is realised, I love the work for its own sake. I do not ask more than that I may be assured that I may look to a maximum salary in the same scale as other considerable charities pay. The City Aid pays its secretary £300 a year. I do not think it would be unfair to suggest to the Committee that I may look to rise to at least £250 and that that sum may be arrived at by yearly increments and so be reached within a short period.

The Committee will, I am sure, understand that the position I hold is a responsible one and needs a good deal of specialised knowledge and experience. I have now a considerable staff to organise and oversee. My mind is continually at work, not without success, to increase the scope and usefulness of the Union and to interest the public.

In addition to this, I do a good deal of the detail work myself. For instance, I paid about two thousand visits last year. Indeed, I find my time very fully occupied and my mind is rarely at rest from the problems which the work presents.

Of this I make no complaint. That work is the best part of my life. And I only draw attention to these fact in order to justify this letter, which I hope will receive friendly and sympathetic consideration."

Although he was, by this time, well supported in his work by paid staff and volunteers, these documents combine to give a clear picture of Frank's vital role in the success of the Cripples Union. Here was an able and energetic man, at the height of his powers, performing prodigious feats of organisation and personal effort with great success for very little money. There can be no doubt that his employers, who must have known his situation very well, were exploiting him.

He would have been aware that every penny that he was paid reduced the amount available to spend on those who were suffering: perhaps this is why the letter to Mr Bryson does not seem to have been sent. At any rate, there is no trace of a reply.

In any case, the question of his pay was shortly, for the Mathews, to become much less pressing. Arthur Holden, who had been staying at Letchworth with Winifred, died, aged 77, in the late summer of 1913 and Evelyn came into her inheritance. The amount was not vast but it was enough, for a time, to support the lifestyle they felt appropriate.

After he left the Cripples Union Frank never took another paid job though he was forced to ask for an honorarium at one point and the expense of his car, which was mainly used for work, was largely provided for. He continued to draw a salary while he remained with the Union, however. Perhaps he thought of it as back pay.

1909 – 1922
THE WOODLANDS AND THE FORELANDS

A short time after his marriage, probably in 1906, Frank gave a talk about the Cripples Union the text of which, annotated in Evelyn's handwriting, has survived.

"In many ways I am one of the most unsuitable persons to talk about crippled children, spending as I have done for nine years, my whole time amongst or working for (them)…I have become so used to their limitations and their deformities, that I cannot realise them as others do, and now and again when I hear people say what a terribly sad sight our big Christmas party in the Town Hall is I find myself inclined to turn round and say 'what nonsense you are talking' for at a party I only see some hundreds of radiantly happy faces.

The very first thing I had to learn when I took up this work 9 years ago was not to see the misery, not to think about the work I could not do, not to think about the deformities, and sufferings of these little people, only to think of how they could be mitigated, how those who were curable could be cured, and those who were incurable could be made happier, to what extent those who were deformed could be educated and enabled to earn their living in the world, and how, approximately, to put them on the same footing as other children….

…You will ask 'what have you done for these little people?' The first, and most important is this, we have discovered them, we have shown that they are there. Nine years ago we knew but 80, today we know over 1,000.

Our first attempt was to bring some happiness into their lives, and we established a special fund to provide them with parties of which there were four every year. This was very necessary for they were confined to their homes year in and year out and could not go…anywhere that ordinary children went. I wish you could see the Town Hall at Christmas, the tables full almost to overflowing with the crippled children who can sit to table while, under the galleries, there are rows of spinal carriages filled with little people who are unable to do anything but lie. 'What a sad sight' people say to me, but I always ask them to look at the children's radiantly happy faces…

…We found these children as a class were friendless and were not getting anything like the attention and help they needed, so the first thing the Society did was to provide a Visitor who would visit every child regularly and know it as far as was possible. Every child in the Society is known by him ((Frank himself)) and he endeavours to make the child and its parents feel that he is their friend to whom they can always turn for advice and who will come to see them regularly…

…In many cases hospital notes are needed: we are always, or nearly always, able to get or help to get them. Then come the instruments, high boots etc, to enable the children to walk better. These we help to get by means of hospital notes or else pay for them and the parents pay the money back so much per week….Then there are other children, the spinal children, who have to lie for two years quite flat on a board, and sometimes longer than two years. These are very sad cases and yet we are able to supply spinal carriages, which they may keep until they are cured, and so they are able to get out into the fresh air and enjoy life instead of always living in one small room with small hope of cure.

One of the first things we had to do was to open a convalescent home. We found our little folk needed in almost every case a long stay in the country. Some of them needed years. There was nowhere where we could send them where they could stay just as long as was necessary. It is right in the heart of the country and there they romp and play just like other children…..I could take up an afternoon telling you about the home, especially about the new one we want to build, but I must hurry on….

I have not told you how we have got twenty children to walk who never had walked before, how we have a teacher who goes round to the homes of the older children who are too delicate to go to work and teaches them basket work and fancy work thus enabling them to earn 5/- or 6/- per week. Nor have I told you of those who we are able to find work for in the ordinary way or by opportunity, nor have I told you how much we are obliged to leave undone for lack of funds…..indeed, I am not exaggerating in the least when I say, as I said when I commenced, I dare not think of the work I leave undone or I could not go through my daily round of work at all."

Frank's passion is as clear as it was in his sermon "Crippled Bairns" given seven or eight years earlier but by the time he came to give this talk he had, obviously, developed his ideas a great deal. He had also learned that he had to discipline his emotions if his efforts were to be productive.

By the time George Cadbury made his gift of The Woodlands, late in 1907, the working methods of the Union had become well established. They had evolved, following Frank's ideas, over more than a decade, from being a good hearted attempt to make life a little better for children suffering from crippling disease to a systematic approach which aimed to prevent the diseases from taking hold, to slow their progress, to cure the children where possible and to help those who could not be restored to full health to gain employment and lead full lives.

The gift of "The Woodlands" promised to satisfy the Union's need for a place where a sufficient number of patients could be sent for long term treatment but work had to be done before it was ready. A lot more money was needed to pay for adaptations and it took several years to bring it to its full potential. It was opened in May 1909 after a thorough overhaul of the house and the adaptation of some outbuildings as open air wards. In the first year there were 37 beds occupied and 58 children were treated.

The thirteenth Annual Report (1912) lists the methods used by the Union and shows how they had continued to evolve.

"Systematic visiting and reports;
Lending spinal carriages and bath chairs for a very small charge;
Giving Hospital and Dispensary notes;
Sending cripples away to the Woodlands and other Homes;
Granting milk or other nourishments free, or at a small charge;
Finding work for some;
Teaching home-bound adults some light handicrafts;
Giving parties and entertainments in winter and summer."

The methods still fall into the three categories of discovery, treatment and after care that Frank described in his talk though the activity of visiting had developed a great deal as an adjunct to medical treatment. The most dramatic change had come about with the opening of the Woodlands

Frank devoted a great deal of his time and energy to visiting, making two or three thousand visits each year for more than twenty years. As time went on three and then two more paid visitors were trained to assist him. The work is well described at the opening of the fourteenth Annual Report (1913):

"....The Secretary spends the greater part of his time in visiting personally and superintending the work of the Visitors. Voluntary Visitors are doing most valuable work, and more are needed, but it has been found by experience that it is only by having trained Visitors in addition that the best results are obtained....It is found that the mothers often do not understand exactly how to carry out the doctors' orders as to treatment, or as to the use of an instrument, and they value greatly a visit from someone who has time to explain difficulties.

It is the province of the Cripples' Union to do this and to see that the doctors' orders are carried out. It is no uncommon thing for one of our staff to be successful in persuading parents to let their child continue with an instrument which they have been about to throw on one side, or to get them to resume it after it has been left off. Above all is this supervision most necessary in cases of tuberculous disease of the joints. There a properly applied splint is absolutely essential to cure and prevent deformity....

...We are glad to say that there is little wilful neglect these days, though the staff still have to combat, day after day, ignorance and stupidity. This is overcome by first gaining the friendship of those they have to advise, and then persistently urging the necessary treatment. Then our work is by no means confined to the crippled one of the family, but often includes other members....

...Apart from teaching the use and necessity of instruments, our visitors are continually explaining the importance of open windows, early bedtime, and suitable diet for children, and hardly a week goes by without some report having been sent to the Medical Officer of Health as to insanitary conditions in connection with the visited homes, such as damp houses, blocked drains, uncovered refuse, etc."

* * *

Tubercular bone disease was much the most common crippling disease among the poor of Birmingham. In the early twentieth century there was no effective drug treatment: the standard treatment was a long period of rest in a healthy environment, such as a sanatorium, presumably in the hope that the body would be strengthened enough to cope with the infection. This was not always successful but cures were often achieved after a year or more of rest. Shorter periods could bring about considerable improvement.

Sanatorium treatment, though preferred, was relatively expensive but, more importantly, the number of beds available within easy reach of Birmingham was nowhere near enough to look after the hundred or more new cases that were being discovered each year. Hence the appeals, from the early years of the Union, for money to build a nursing home. Until that could be achieved the Union had been obliged to do what it could, even if that meant that most of the children remained for most of the time in their homes, perhaps with short periods at the cottage home at Chadwick End. The development of the Woodlands from 1909 very soon made a great difference.

The build up was rapid. In the fourth year (1912-13) the number of beds was increased to 60. 137 children were sent there, of whom 50 went for three weeks. The remainder were judged to need long treatment. 38 children who had received long treatment went home, the majority of them cured.

Two years later again (1914-15) there were 70 children at "The Woodlands". George Cadbury had presented a new ward but, it was said, at least another 20 beds were needed. "The Woodlands" had been recognised as a Special Open Air School and almost all the children over five years of age were having several hours of school daily and "there is a very happy spirit of work amongst the children, who look forward eagerly to their lessons, which give them a new interest in life, and there can be little doubt that in these cases of surgical tuberculosis there is a much greater hope of recovery for those whose minds are healthily occupied and whose days are filled with happy work and play."

In the same report Frank is starting to formulate the next advance in the scheme of treatment – convalescent and boarding out work.

"The amount spent on this work increases year by year as there are quite a substantial number of children who, even after a long stay at Woodlands, still need a few months in the country before being sent to their homes. There are others who are not ill enough to go to Woodlands and need some months, occasionally some years, in the country to aid or complete their cure. During the year we have had more than six children staying at various cottages in Knowle village…

…For a long time the Committee have been exercised in their minds as to this boarding out work. It is difficult in many cases to get adequate supervision, and the children get no education. They have been considering the advisability of starting an open air sanatorium in the country…

…The cost of maintenance for 20 children would be very little more than the present boarding out system…The scheme would also have another great advantage, as it would be possible to pass children out of Woodlands more quickly. Once children have passed the recumbency stage they do not need skilled nursing, and it has been found that tubercular children readily respond to change of air and scene."

Although the work of the Union was able to continue without interruption during the period of hostilities, the first world war did put a stop to any major building projects. Nevertheless, the idea of a purpose built convalescent home was mentioned again in the next report (1916) and, at length, two years later when it was revealed that an anonymous donor had given the £2,500 proceeds from the sale of his house, leading the Committee to think that it would be possible to start building as soon as war restrictions were removed.

The next year (1918-19), however, it was found that the increase in building costs over the war years meant that the desired home would cost twice as much as had been thought. However, a site had been found, negotiations for its purchase were under way and the Committee appealed for another £3,000, assuring subscribers that "money could not be better invested than in the prevention of deformity in the next generation."

In the meantime, the Union found itself short of accommodation. Beds it had been using at the orthopaedic hospital and sanatorium at Baschurch in Shropshire were needed for local use. £500 was withdrawn from the building fund, hitherto devoted to the upkeep of the fabric at Woodlands, and used to build two new wards there with 18 beds. The Woodlands as a whole was thriving. By the end of the year 1918-19, 95 beds were open and a few months later 104. The report for that year goes on:

"The results obtained are more than satisfactory, and although the numbers have increased so much we have been able to keep it free from Institutionalism. The children have a natural home life there, keeping rabbits, going excursions with the recreation teacher to the parks and country around; visiting the Art Gallery and Markets in Birmingham, and paying the expenses of these outings out of their own pocket money. The results of the savings bank, too, have been very encouraging.

To interest the parents in their children's education a special School Day was arranged one Saturday afternoon in May. The parents were able to attend and watch the children being taught, and to see their lessons and exercise books. This experiment is very successful and it is hoped to make it even more so on future occasions.

The Nursery School is proving a great success as well as a pleasure for the little ones, whose curriculum is by no means too strenuous. For the Nursery School and the younger children in the ordinary classes a set of Montessori appliances has been purchased, and although it is impossible to apply the Montessori teaching in its entirety in a Hospital School, it has been very satisfactorily adapted."

This was the twentieth annual report of the Union: it starts with a summary of the growth in activities over the eight years since the work at the Woodlands got under way. Over that period the number of patients on the books had remained roughly constant at around 1400 but expenditure had increased from £3,472 to £12,256 reflecting both a fall in the value of money and the great enhancement in the level of treatment that had become possible. Beds at the Woodlands had more than doubled in number and a school with five teachers had opened, bringing in a grant of £1,700. The number of Visitors had increased from four to eight and the amount spent on surgical appliances had increased from £55 to £885. Expenditure on children's convalescent work, apart from that at Woodlands had increased from £62 to £1,760.

Over the same period there had been a considerable growth in the amount of income coming from working people, including the patients' families. Parents' payments had risen from £190 to £1,638 and money collected voluntarily by parents had risen to £470. The Workmen's Auxiliary Committee, had handed over £1,748 and a newly formed Women's Guild, made up of the mothers of patients, had raised £30. Altogether, almost two thirds of the total income came from working people in sharp contrast to the early days when the Union depended almost entirely on middle class charity. It had always been Frank's policy to involve the patients, their families and the community around them in all aspects of the Union's activities and he was rightly proud of this demonstration of their support and self reliance.

Commenting on this growth the report goes on:

> "The results of this huge expenditure of money are so slow that only those who are actively engaged in the work can see them clearly, but we can confidently say that as a result of our 20 years work there is an enormous decrease in deformity, especially among the crippled CHILDREN of our city."

In Frank's customary style an example is given, this time it is the history
"of a little boy, D. S.

Denis was born with shockingly deformed feet. He came to us when nineteen days old, was seen by our surgeon, and treatment commenced immediately. He was in plaster cases for about five months and his feet were improving nicely, when he had a serious illness and was unable to go on with treatment. He was ill for several months and his feet relapsed considerably. When able to have treatment again his feet were put in strapping, and he had to be seen daily. He was steadily improving when he developed pneumonia and had to go into the Children's Hospital. Treatment had again to be discontinued for six months. It was then necessary to send him to Baschurch to have an operation. He went in June 1916 and had an operation on both feet a fortnight later. He was again so ill that his life was despaired of, but with very great care and attention he recovered and steadily improved. He remained at Baschurch until December, 1917 when he returned home. He attended the Office Clinic weekly and his feet were in plaster cases until December 1918, when they were removed and ordinary boots and irons applied. These he is still wearing and will continue to do so for a short time, merely as a safeguard against relapse, as his feet are perfectly straight and well developed, and he is growing into quite a bonny boy."

He goes on:

"Spinal disease is robbed of its worst terror, for deformity is almost entirely done away with where it is properly treated; and we are increasingly able to treat it properly. The same applies to the deformity arising from hip disease, and if we are able to continue the progress we are making the high cork boot will be rare in the next generation of Birmingham cripples.

In cases where the deformity arises from rickets nearly all of it can be obliterated. Where it is due to paralysis (the second most common crippling condition) it can be very greatly improved; but the amount of money and time needed is enormous, and the Cripples' Union has hardly touched the fringe of this work. For paralytic children a special hospital is needed, and if we had this it would be possible to benefit a vast number of children for whom at present we can do little.

We would repeat what we have said in our appeals so often, that the prevention of deformity in children is almost entirely a matter of money and time"

He then appeals for capital, to build the proposed convalescent home and a special hospital for the treatment of paralysis, for funds to open offices and a clinic in the centre of the city, for the endowment of beds at the Woodlands and for a doubling of annual income.

His appeal for the first of this ambitious list seems to have succeeded for on October 5th 1921 the Lord Mayor of Birmingham officially opened the "Forelands" Convalescent School for Crippled Children near Bromsgrove.

Forelands and its 18 acre estate had been bought in 1920 for £8,000. This, and the cost of much of the structural work needed to provide accommodation, was paid for from the proceeds of a special appeal by the Birmingham Mail Christmas Tree Fund which raised £15,000. The Ministry of Health also made a grant towards the capital cost which amounted, altogether, to about £25,000. Both the Ministry and the Birmingham City Medical Officer of Health expressed their approval of the methods of open-air treatment for crippled children adopted at the Forelands.

The house itself was made to serve as an administration block with accommodation for staff and a main dining room for the children while, on high ground opposite two open-air dormitories, each with 40 beds, were linked by a school block also open along one side.

Practically all of the children's time was to be spent in the open air. When they were not in bed and not in school they had their own garden plots and also assisted the gardener, kept chickens and looked after pigeons and rabbits and played strenuous games. In wet weather they played in the former coach house which had been extended to form a covered play ground closed on three sides.

The first children had been admitted to the Forelands on November 2nd 1920 when building work had only just started. By the time of the formal opening the School had its full complement of 80 children with a staff of 17 under a "Lady Superintendent". They included a sister in charge and four nurses, five teachers, one qualified in gardening and poultry keeping, a housekeeper and five maids.

The opening took place a month after Frank's fiftieth birthday and he must have felt at the time that it represented a culmination of his work for the Cripples Union. He had led it from small beginnings as a group of people trying to improve the lives of fewer than a hundred children to an organisation employing dozens of staff, some working in its two institutions, others, including himself, working to seek out sufferers and to provide family support and training for more than a thousand children and adults on the Union's books.

While he had been developing an organisation and a set of methods to deal with the existing problems of crippling diseases among children the evolution of society had begun to create conditions in which the problems would no longer arise. In Birmingham the City Council pursued a policy of improving housing conditions that would accelerate in the years after the end of the war. Nationally, the Liberal governments of Asquith and Lloyd George had made a beginning of a welfare state and generally, despite setbacks, the nation became increasingly prosperous. The conditions of grinding poverty and wide scale slum housing that Frank had always believed to be the root causes of the diseases were gradually disappearing.

He had forced his fellow citizens to recognise the problems of crippling disease among the poor of the city and to do something about them. The Union was widely supported by rich and poor and was well recognised by officialdom. It was now able to work on a scale that was commensurate with the problem and would eventually solve it. With this growth in scale had necessarily come a need for accountability which was satisfied by the rise of a bureaucracy headed by voluntary committees.

Frank always had been, and would remain, uncomfortable with committees and all that went with them. It seems overwhelmingly likely that all the committees he had to deal with in the course of his work held him in the highest regard and supported him wholeheartedly but his instinctive view of the urgency of the work made him impatient of the speed that committees work and intolerant of the need to carry his committee with him wherever he wanted to go.

Frank's strengths were in working outside the government system, in mobilising people to work for a common aim and in organising them effectively. But the Cripples Union he had created by the early 1920's had become as much part of the system as it was possible for a charity to be – and in those days it was the norm for social and health care to be organised on a charitable basis. He could see that the work that only he could do was complete.

He must have realised too, at some level, that it would soon be time for him to move on, because he would not be able to sustain the pace of his work for much longer.

Also, in the offing, was the question of the relationship between the Cripples Union and the Royal Orthopaedic and Spinal Hospital in Birmingham.

The hospital had been founded as a result of a meeting of concerned gentlemen in June 1817, called under the chairmanship of the Earl of Dartmouth, to consider the "Propriety of establishing an Institution for the Relief of Persons labouring under Bodily Deformity" (Maurice White, 1997). It was readily established that the need for a hospital existed and a committee was formed.

This led swiftly to the establishment of a list of subscribers whose contributions would support the provision of this service to people who could not afford to pay. The charity had to find the money for premises, nursing and supporting staff and medical and surgical supplies. At least some of the doctors gave their services free but even with their donation the committee found it very difficult to make ends meet even for a hospital working on the smallest scale.

In return for their support subscribers had the right to nominate a certain number of prospective patients, using a system of the "hospital notes" type. The number of notes allowed for a given subscription had to be adjusted from time to time to balance supply and demand.

By the time of the formation of the Cripples Union the Hospital, though perennially short of money, was well established. It was natural division of functions for it to be the centre for surgery and medicine for crippled children and for the Cripples Union to make it possible for the treatment to be carried out for those children whose parents had not enough money to pay. As time went on the Union's resources increased to the point where it became the main provider of inpatient facilities for children, even providing beds for the Hospital to use.

The Union had always had its own medical advisers, usually drawn from among the doctors serving the hospital, and it seems, from Frank's words quoted above, that it sometimes, at least in later years, took over the whole function of diagnosis, treatment and convalescence.

There was a great potential for overlap. This probably didn't matter too much when neither the Hospital nor the Union could do more than work away at the fringes of the problem. But as it came to look possible to deal with all crippling disease among the City's children it must have seemed to make more and more sense to combine the Institutions.

Negotiations about closer cooperation between them were under way as early as 1920 but do not seem to have got anywhere at that time. However, Frank must have been able to see that merger was inevitable and that his freedom to work in the way he thought right would be curtailed. This seems to have been a major factor in his decision to resign.

Maurice White records that on January 3rd 1922 he wrote to Miss E L Rolason, the Honorary Secretary of The Cripples Union reminding her that he had warned her a year and a half previously that he was contemplating giving up the work of the Cripples Union and telling her that he had decided to send in his resignation. He cited the likely decision to carry out the merger as one reason but referred also to the strain he had been feeling as a result of the increasing pace and weight of the work.

There is no doubt that Frank was firmly of the view, at this point, that it was time for him to go. But his personal feelings were mixed. There were still important things on his agenda for the Cripples Union, such as a sustained attack on the crippling effects of paralysis and the letter does suggest that his decision might have been different and his departure delayed if he had had his way about the future of the Union, especially with regard to the question of merger with the Hospital.

It is not surprising that he was finding the work stressful and it is true that he used holiday breaks as a way of coping with stress throughout his life. But there is little to suggest that he was too much troubled by stress when things were going well. It seems likely, therefore, that it was not the hard work that was worrying him so much as a feeling that he was being cast aside for the sake of progress that he did not entirely endorse.

He was not in any hurry to take up a new line of endeavour. His resignation letter suggests that he was thinking of moving from Birmingham and starting work for crippled children elsewhere but it was a full year before he started his next charity. He had first to overcome the effect on him of what he felt was a rejection. Then, rather than move his home, he and Evelyn stayed where they were and he used the organisational techniques he had developed to work for children who he saw as suffering from an invisible form of crippling caused by the precursors of heart disease.

His committee at the Cripples Union noted his decision to leave in unambiguous terms, recording his unique contribution to its development and achievements and paying tribute to his devotion and untiring work.

But it would have been a poor tribute if they had not got on with the development of the work in the way the members felt best. With Frank gone they were able to complete a merger with the Hospital within three years, probably relieved not to have to upset him further. The result still prospers, at the Woodlands, as the Birmingham Royal Orthopaedic Hospital NHS Trust, the Forelands having been closed in 1986.

Frank did not, by any means, lose touch. He was to recruit supporters and staff for his new enterprises from among those who had helped him in the Cripples Union and from among former patients and staff and he was present at a bed endowment ceremony at the Woodlands as late as 1947, the year before he died. His achievement with the Cripples Union formed, perhaps, the peak of his career in terms of the mountains that he was able to move and it would have been understandable in anyone else having got to that height if they had subsequently rested on their laurels. But Frank was not made that way and, after a year's break, he started again.

1922 – 1937 INVALID CHILDREN

Frank's Chronology says that he left the Cripples Union on March 31st 1922 and that he started the Invalid Children's Society (The Birmingham Society for the Care of Invalid Children) in March 1923.

It would have been perfectly reasonable for him to take a year's holiday. He had been working at a rate that would have exhausted any normal person, he had found himself in a stressful opposition to his colleagues over the future of the Cripples Union and he had been complaining about the effect that his situation was having on his health.

It is known that at some time during the year he went "to help out" at Plympton in Devon. This may have been in connexion with the work of the Plymouth and District branch of the Crippled Children's Aid Association – he later used the back of some of their unused headed paper to make notes. There is also a suggestion at some point that he would go to the United States, though this seems to have come to nothing. By September 1922 the Mathews were in Llwyngwryl where they seem to have remained for several months.

Whatever the public front it is clear that Frank was very upset and depressed about his departure from the Cripples Union. The evidence for this comes from a set of almost twenty documents, obviously in Evelyn's hand, which purport to be communications from Frank's and her parents obtained, it would seem, by a method of automatic writing during spiritualist séances.

Ina Taylor has written of the Holdens' interest in spiritualism, in parallel with their strongly held Unitarianism. Arthur Holden had written on thought transference and believed he had evidence of it in his wife's ability in automatic writing without, apparently, any knowledge of its content.

In the years before Evelyn's marriage the household witnessed weekly séances with friends and visiting mediums taking part, Mrs Holden herself being considered a particularly good medium. Evelyn's three oldest sisters all took active parts though Evelyn is said never to have really involved herself and to have said later that it frightened her and that she felt it was best left alone. Obviously, therefore, she must have felt that there was something in it.

The idea of communicating with the dead using spiritualist methods had been accepted by many, most famously by Sir Oliver Lodge, one of Frank's earliest supporters, during and immediately after the first world war. It was, as it were, in the air and it is not surprising that Evelyn seems to have turned to spiritualism as a way of comforting and supporting Frank when he left the Cripples Union.

Some of Frank's earliest recorded reading, in 1890 at about the time he first knew the Holdens, was of books about spiritualism. He would have been familiar with the ideas and, as his later correspondence was to show, included some of them in his general belief about life and death. At a time of distress he would have been likely to accept the idea that his parents could offer comfort through Evelyn.

Several of the documents are marked with date and place and it may be that the séances started while Frank and Evelyn were at Llwygwryl. Ethel would have been there too and may well have encouraged the attempt to help her brother even if she did not necessarily subscribe to the method – Frank once described her as "devious".

What is probably the first is undated. It reads as follows:

"My dear I've been hoping that you would give me the chance of writing to you, for when your mind is so distraught I cannot get 'through' to you by speech. You must both put out of your minds the thought that there is no 'future' before you, and no prospect of happiness. Because none of these things are true. You will travel through this very dark valley before long and it will bring you to a very happy country where you will find calmness and peace, useful work and love surrounding you.

Put these dark thoughts away from you, refuse to think them. Frank will find that this last blow will not have the far reaching results that he thinks it will – there are years of happy and useful work before him yet. You must have faith in my words my dears, because they will help you through these hard times if you will give them entrance and belief.

I wish for your sakes that I could be more definite – that I could give you dates and place, although such particulars could not give me greater certainty of the outcome, it would help you I know. But it cannot be.

And this next thing, I know, will sound an easy thing to say from where I am, but much more difficult for you to perform down among the inelect. You must put littleness of persons away from you. That is the only real harm that anyone can do. To so act that we are smaller than our ideal stature. It is only in letting ourselves be little ourselves that any harm can come to us – No event can bring us harm otherwise, however hard or unjust circumstances or people may seem.

Put away anger and resentment – they are moral poisons polluting our natures and taking away from us clear sight. My dear ones it is such acute suffering as this that gives you your opportunity to win those spiritual victories that can never come through unalloyed happiness – I want my dear ones, and you are both very dear to me, to gain such a triumph that they will feel afterwards this suffering was worth while. I believe that that is going to be but it must be by trampling on the worst in yourselves, not in others. Do not seek revenge my darlings, be as magnanimous as you know how to be. Courage my dears and patience yet a little while. Your loving Mother.

You are in too disturbed a state to get anything through from an unaccustomed source."

Taken out of its spiritualist context this letter reads like the advice any sensible and sensitive wife might give to a distressed husband. It is coherent and well written especially considering that it must have been written out at a sitting with no opportunity for correction or revision. Were it not for the context it would be tempting to put it down as a subterfuge, a method by which Evelyn thought she could reinforce her support for Frank But what followed makes it seem certain that, whatever unconscious influence Evelyn's own thoughts and feelings may have had on the content, she genuinely believed that they were a result of supernatural influences.

The earliest dated document, of September 10th 1922, starts with a passage in the same hand as its predecessor, quite close to Evelyn's conscious writing, but with nonsensical interruptions:

> "My dear ones. It is very delightful to greet you in these happy surroundings, where you meet with such welcome and affection and I shall like to have you here to gain help for future work ((squiggle)) At the same time it is not easy to write where there are so many influences close at hand. Another time let us talk together out of doors, where it is quiet and peaceful and where there is nothing to disturb or conflict. It is a little like the difficulties of this new ((situation)), where one current is apt to obstruct another one.

> If you knew how delicate are the conditions that surround communication you would not wonder at the many mistakes and blunders that are made, nor would you wonder at the trivialities which are mentioned, because such are ((easier – deleted)) the readiest interchange of talk whether it be on this side or on ((this – deleted)) your side. It is this glibness of "small change that is such an obstruction to the discussion of things which really matter and they constantly obtrude themselves here, as there, when trying to harmonise the conditions, so perhaps I ought not to condemn them for they are sometimes of use on both sides ((Then too, one may perhaps lay too much stress - deleted))"

At this point the writing changes becoming stronger and more masculine looking, though still with many of Evelyn's characteristic letter formations:

"((squiggle)) dear boy I cannot say much tonight, only greet you with warm affection and with a word of good cheer. I want you to know that I have watched you and been near you through these past troubled months and that I am indeed grateful to see that the hardest time is behind you and that there is light coming before. I cannot write more tonight but shall come to your next sitting. My love to you and to this wife of yours whom I am very glad to be able to greet in that capacity for she has been a help and a stay to you in the hour of trial. Your loving father Dan Mathews."

The last dated letter, of 17th June 1923 was produced several weeks after the Mathews had returned to Bournville and the new Society had started its work:

"My dears. You see than Frank's work is making a good start and he will find that he will overcome any difficulty with regard to the Beds. He can go forward with absolute trust that the plan of work will unfold continuously and with very few hitches. I foresee a very happy and useful time ahead. And I am glad that he felt he could join in yesterday's activities. It is a very great thing to put aside the attitude of bitterness, as well as the thing itself. He will feel all the happier in his mind for it and gain a greater serenity."

There is no obvious sign that any of the undated documents were produced before September 1922 or after June 1923, though when a plausible sequence, based on content, is constructed there is a suggestion that the move to Plymouth came after the stay at Llwyngwryl. It looks as though the Mathews may have left Birmingham in mid 1922 with neither a decision about what to do in future nor any clear intention of ever returning – though the house was not given up.

What is clear, though, is the intensity of support that Evelyn was giving Frank in his time of doubt and the encouragement she gave him in overcoming the teething troubles of the new Society. Nothing has come to light to suggest that the Mathews ventured into spiritualistic manifestations in the eighteen years between their wedding and Frank's leaving the Cripples Union. In his later correspondence Frank refers, as will be seen, to spiritualist ideas but there is no evidence of any more séances. By the end of June 1923 the new Society was starting to operate successfully and the need for supernatural support may be assumed to have disappeared. It seems that they only happened in this one period of disappointment and uncertainty.

* * *

The new Society's first Annual report (March 1923 – March 1924) includes a foreword in which Frank explains how he came to start it:

"My twenty five years' experience in visiting crippled children in all parts of the City very early caused me to realise that alongside the problem with which I was dealing ran another which was equally grave – the problem of children suffering from serious illnesses such as Rheumatism, Chorea (St Vitus Dance), and Heart Disease.

Indeed, during the first ten years some attempt was made to deal with children suffering from Chorea and Heart Disease, but it was soon found impracticable, as the problem of the crippled child was a specialised one and could not be further complicated, so it seemed fitting that when the time came for me to relinquish the post of Secretary to the Cripples' Union, some effort should be made to cope with this problem....

...We must realise that Heart Disease is by far the greatest cause of death at the present day. Last year 59,800 people died of this ailment in England and Wales. That is to say that one death in every eight is due to Heart Disease. The majority of cases of Heart Disease commence in childhood, and are frequently unnoticed at their onset. If cases are dealt with promptly in their earlier stages a cure can be usually effected. But once the heart is seriously damaged complete recovery is impossible.

Rheumatism and Chorea are the two most frequent causes of Heart Disease....

....It is generally considered by members of the medical profession dealing with these cases that Rheumatism and Chorea in children are almost entirely diseases of poverty, so that a Society such as this, which comes into contact with individual cases, and helps to procure the means of treatment and cure, may well be the channel by which those who realise the gravity of the need may be helped to relieve it…"

Conditions in 1923 were different from those of the 1890s when the Cripples' Union was started. There had been progress in alleviating the worst effects of poverty, partly because of social legislation leading to better welfare provision and partly because real incomes generally had risen.

Also, there were others in the City already working on the problem of heart disease in children. The Education Committee already had twenty seven beds in use at its Baskerville House and had plans to double the number. Several of the City's hospitals also had programmes. However, Dr A P Thompson, Medical Officer of the City's Special Schools had estimated that at least 150 beds were needed to deal with the matter adequately: there was no shortage of opportunity to help. Moreover, Frank believed that his was the only organisation devoted to preventing damage by developing heart disease by attacking its precursors.

The treatment was, essentially, supervised rest and care in healthy surroundings. In the first report it was regretted that, although the society was formed in April it had been impossible to get active work under way until the beginning of August as it took some time to find suitable places to which to send the children. Nevertheless, in the eight remaining months over 100 children were sent away to country hospitals and convalescent homes or were boarded out at farms or cottages in the country. It was noted that the boarding out, under Frank's supervision, had been forced on the Society by a shortage of hospital beds and was regarded as experimental but so far had had encouraging results. Sixty six of the children sent away had been suffering from Chorea. None of them had less than three months' treatment and the majority six months.

The regretted delay not withstanding, it is clear that the work got off to a rapid start: Frank would have been comfortable to be working with only a few willing helpers and was never in the habit of allowing the grass to grow under his feet. Together, they must have done a lot of preparation.

He was well supported by his family and friends. Evelyn was a member of the first Committee and the work of the Society was conducted, for the first three years from an office set up at 47 Maple Road. Evelyn was joined later by Myra Wynn Thomas from Cripples' Union days.

Frank's sisters, Pauline and Ethel, and his aunt Charlotte Vose Solomon were among the first year's list of subscribers, giving 15s, £1, and £1/1/1 respectively, as was the firm of Arthur Holden and Sons. Bernard Holden became an individual subscriber a year later.

While he was at the Cripples Union Frank had set up a small typing school under one of the senior patients, Florrie West, who also became a member of his new Committee. When he left the Union the girls of the typing school formed the Ivy Fellowship to help him in his new work. Later, they were joined by others including Hilda Price, a friend of Florrie West, and Gwen Hazelwood both of whom were to become important contributors to Frank's story.

The Fellowship, identified by Frank in the report as "a group of old friends", raised the £20 needed to equip the office and offered much encouragement and help in starting the Society. They met two or three times a year and continued to support Frank's work by donating cash, helping with house to house collections, and organising an annual gala sale at Selly Manor in Bournville.

The first report also thanks the Misses Mathews, Pauline and Ethel, who "enabled the Society to be started by raising the sum of £30 by an American Tea." What an American Tea might be is not explained but it must have been quite a grand event to have raised so large an amount. Ethel is also thanked for taking four children for a month at her cottage at Llwyngwril.

Howard Rolason, whose wife was another member of the first Committee is thanked for much encouragement and help and for raising £30 in subscriptions. Members of that family had been listed among the subscribers to the Cripples' Union for many years.

The first year's income was £729, mostly in donations but also including a grant of £58 from the United Services Fund and £81 in payment by parents toward the cost of sending children away. £409 was spent on maintaining children and £103 on office furniture and expenses, the balance of income over expenditure, it was explained, lest donors should feel tempted to rest on their laurels, "having been paid by donors in advance for cases already under treatment, so that for every fresh case further funds must be raised."

In only the Society's second Annual Report Frank starts to make a case for a country convalescent school. Commenting on a letter in which Dr A P Thomson, Medical Officer of the Birmingham Special Schools estimates the number of children in the city with some sort of heart disease of rheumatic origin to be about 3000, he says

"...no less than 1,500 ((of the 3,000)) will die before they are forty. Yet if the facilities for cure existed, out of these 1,500, 90 percent might be cured. At present the facilities for cure are little more than a decimal point. We must remember that heart disease is by far the greatest cause of death in the present day. No less than one death in every eight is due to this. However one looks at it, whether from the point of view of the family or of the waste to the community, this seems a terrible tragedy, and there is irony in the fact that there is an empty ward in the Children's Hospital which might be devoted to this valuable work if only the means were forthcoming.

If such a ward, and the splendid work done at Baskerville, could be supplemented by a Convalescent School in the country, a firm foundation would have been laid for future work....

Our object in dealing with these children is to make certain of cure, so that although the number sent away has not been greatly increased, the length of stay has been increased to a minimum of six months. The stay has been seldom less than nine months, and in quite a number of cases it has been fifteen months and the children still away….

Our Boarding-out work has improved greatly during the year….As far as possible we are placing the children on small farms as we find that in this way they get ample diet with plenty of milk Equally important, all the year round there is something to interest them All the children are weighed fortnightly and inspected by our Hon. Secretary….

In connection with the Boarding-out we would for two reasons emphasise our previous remarks as to the need for a Convalescent School to take the place of this side of the work:

At present the children are getting no education during their long stay in the country

The supervision, which means fortnightly visits, involving as it does nearly 6,000 miles a year, takes a great deal of money and time, which might be spent on developing the society."

Frank was a skilful and resourceful fund raiser. He took what he thought they could afford from the families of the children he was helping and encouraged them to help bring in more money – the Annual reports usually carried advertisements for things made by the children or their families, furniture polish for example. Some other activities have already been mentioned. But the bedrock support came from subscriptions and donations that were solicited by all means including hand written appeal letters produced to a standard text by volunteers.

As a result the income of the Society grew steadily, its income more than doubling to £1,790 in the second year and increasing again to £2,771 in the third, the latter including a large donation of £145 from Winifred Holden which Frank set aside in a special fund for a convalescent home. Thereafter it increased year by year until, in the Society's tenth year (1932-33) ordinary income had reached £4,709 and the Society also received a legacy of £771.

This increase was the result of much effort that had to be housed somewhere so, in 1927, the front room of 47 Maple Road having been outgrown, offices were rented, at first at 6 Linden Road and later at 65 Elm Road, both within a few hundred yards of the Mathews' house.

The fourth year's report describes a couple of cases that give a flavour of the conditions under which childhood illnesses were developing and of the way the Society sought to overcome their effects:

"…"F.E.", a little boy of 10 years, who had severe chorea and was very anaemic. The chorea was so bad that, for a considerable time after he was in hospital, he was thought to be mentally deficient. He is one of a family of three children and his father was out of work. He lives in a house in a narrow street, and shut in at the back by a very high wall, so that neither at the back or front was there an adequate supply of air or light. The parents are respectable people, but they had no chance of getting him well there. He was at Much Wenlock (Lady Forrester Memorial Hospital) for 12 months and improved considerably. All the chorea left him. He was then transferred to Blymhill (boarded out), and has been there 11 months. The doctor has just seen him, and reports him fit to be admitted to Uffculme Open-Air School. He is now a strong and healthy little boy.

"E.C." was a little girl of 9 years , who was in hospital with a bad rheumatic heart. She lives in a slum house in a slum street, and would have relapsed immediately had she returned home. Her father was a drunkard, but when in work paid regularly his share of her keep. She, too, was sent to Wenlock for 13 months, and was then transferred to a farm at Tenbury. She has now been there 7 months. Her doctor saw her there recently, and hopes to arrange for her to be transferred to the Open-Air School at Uffculme shortly."

And also a charming letter from "a little boy who wept bitterly on leaving home":

" I am getting on alright and if Mrs. Plevys baby is as fat as a pig we have got a pig here. I want to stop on this farm, we have got a pig a horse named lady and my day of writing is Thursday and thank Mrs. Ford for the comics and Dick. We had two pigs only they killed one to eat and it is on the cratch so I think this is all and send my love to mom and dad, sid, charl, girt, dick, alf, Mrs. Plevy and my love to aunties and uncles. WILLIAM."

The same report notes that the Lord Mayor of Birmingham had become president of the society – a considerable coup – and that it had been necessary to agree an honorarium of £2 per week for the Hon. Secretary in addition to his £100 per year car allowance. It is explained that without this supplement to his income he would have been forced to resign and take a paid post, in which case it would have been necessary to employ a full time secretary at considerable extra expense. This was at a time when economic conditions were very depressed and it seems likely that the family firm on which the Mathews relied for much of their income would have had difficulty maintaining its dividend payments.

The sixth Annual Report (1928-29) summarises the achievements to date. In all, 199 children had been sent away of whom 51 were still away at the time of writing. The length of treatment of those who had returned had been from 6 months to 5 years with the largest number between 6 months and 2 years. 57 were at work and 36 were at school and keeping well. There had been a few choreaic relapses and several cases of children with incurable heart disease, 5 of whom had died. 29 others had been withdrawn from treatment by parents but had seemed to benefit while they were away.

Although the numbers were comparatively small, especially when compared with the number of sufferers, Frank felt that the methods he was using had proved effective and that it was time to return to the question of a convalescent school where children could be treated without forfeiting their education.

He already had £164 in his school fund and two friends, who preferred to remain anonymous, had promised a further £500. The committee of the Society had felt encouraged to advertise for a house to let and had found a suitable place near Warwick, about 20 miles to the south of Birmingham. A further £1,000 would allow them to take the house and thus, as he put it, put the work on a thoroughly sound footing.

In the next year Frank was able to report that "by the end of June 1930 we shall have our own convalescent school at Haseley Hall, near Warwick, which will accommodate forty children, and staff in addition. The house is of sixteen rooms, most of which face south, standing in eighteen acres of ground. It has been provisionally passed by the Board of Education, and is now being altered and adapted." Subscribers and donors had given £1,500, in response to the previous year's appeal, toward furnishings and alterations.

Haseley Hall was a late eighteenth century house which had, most recently, been used by the weighing machine manufacturer W T Avery of Birmingham as a Country Home for senior staff. It is said to have had "four excellent reception rooms, a billiards room, sixteen bedrooms," and a long gallery. The Society took it on a tenancy lease which would expire in 1951.

Owing to a shortage of funds it was decided to open the school for girls only, in the first instance. There would be an education grant which would help toward maintenance and the committee "had been fortunate in being able to appoint as superintendent Miss Moore, who was formerly headmistress at 'Forelands', the well known convalescent school of the Royal Cripples Hospital."

Sadly, Pauline Mathews had died in 1924. However, when Haseley Hall opened in 1930 her aunt and sister were well on the way to finding the £500 that would be needed to endow a bed in her memory. Charlotte Vose Solomon donated £250 in 1929-30 and Ethel raised £83 in the same year. She continued to raise money year by year, finally completing the endowment with a donation of £65 in 1932.

The regime at Haseley is described by Eileen Wilson Smith, one of the teachers (quoted in A Breath of Fresh Air - Birmingham's Open-Air Schools, by Frances Wilmot and Pauline Seal , Phillimore 1998)

"I was at Haseley Hall Hospital School from September 1937 to March 1942 when it was run by the Birmingham Society for the Care of Invalid Children. The school catered for 40 girls between the ages of about eight and fifteen years. All of them suffered from rheumatism and chorea (St Vitus' Dance) and they came mainly from very poor housing conditions in Birmingham. Many houses had no indoor bathrooms and the WCs at the end of the backyards were shared by more than one family. The conditions in which the girls lived gave rise to much illness, especially rheumatic conditions.

The girls come to the school usually for nine months – though some stayed longer if they were not fit to return home. They came on the recommendation of doctors in Birmingham, or sometimes direct from hospital following rheumatic fever, in some cases resulting in rheumatic heart condition. Some girls returned to the school as many as three times while I was there. The Headmistress was Miss Marion A Moore who had trained at Bedford Froebel Training College in Bedford.

Because it was less strain on their hearts, all the girls had to go upstairs backwards, and some of them scuffled upstairs at great speed after a few days! Diet was important and no citrus fruit or other acid fruits were allowed. Breakfast consisted of thin porridge (with milk and sugar stirred into it in the kitchen), followed by half a round of fried bread with a blob of Marmite on it.

There was a system of coloured badges, beginning with white and progressing through silver, yellow, orange, light green, dark green, light blue, dark blue, purple to gold, which meant ready to return home. The school doctor, Dr Mitchell, saw the girls monthly and if they were making normal progress they were promoted to the next coloured badge. Each badge brought with it something extra a girl could do e.g. white, full time in bed; silver, breakfast in bed, up after breakfast but on a chaise longue in school; yellow, up for breakfast and desk and chair in school.

The school had two classes, the younger girls being taught by Miss Priestman and the top class were mine. There were 24 girls in my class and the range of intelligence was very wide. The aim was to try to get each girl up to a standard where she would be able to hold her own in a mainstream school, and the teaching in the three R's was entirely individual. I taught all subjects and took music with each of the two classes. We had singing, bamboo pipe making and playing, and percussion playing.

The nurse who was in charge of the 'home' side of the school was Miss Maud Bigger and there were two housemothers and a housekeeper and the usual kitchen and domestic staff.

The girls were clothed by the school and some of the dresses were distinctly 'orphanage' looking, though gradually more skirts and pullovers were worn in the winter.

In the outbuildings behind the main building the girls had their houses where they played 'families', putting up curtains, cleaning and entertaining in summer evenings and at weekends. There was on the lawn, Martineau Cottage, a revolving summer house which was given by the Martineau family of Knowle and which was a lovely place for a child to sit when not well enough to be in school.

There was a music room at the end of the building where we had our assembly each morning and a service on Sunday mornings, where I played the piano for hymns, took singing lessons and percussion playing.

Croquet was played on the lawns as this was a game which put minimum strain on the heart. As girls became better in health they were allowed to play netball. There was a Guide Company of which Miss Moore was Captain and which I took over when she left; Miss Priestman took Brownies.

We attended Haseley church on alternate Sunday afternoons for the service at 3pm. Miss Moore brought a small group of less well girls in her car but the rest walked along the Birmingham to Warwick Road for about half a mile, and then turned off across the field beside the Falcon Inn to reach the church. There we were met by the Lady of the Manor who lived at Haseley Manor. Together with us, she and her cook made up the entire congregation, seated in the box pews where the smaller girls could see nothing of what was going on!"

Within a couple of years of its opening, Haseley Hall was well established and had been commended for its arrangements and its work by both the Birmingham Medical Officer of Health and the inspector of the Board of Education. It was felt that some children would benefit from being in a smaller group and, of course, Haseley did not take boys – nor did it ever while it was being run by the Society. The 1931-32 Report gives the numbers boarded out at six boys and six girls and notes that recent benefit cuts, coupled with the infamous means test, had led to more families falling below the poverty line. The Society hoped to increase the number boarded out to help cope with growing demand.

Stress was still laid on the after care work – Frank claimed that the Society was the only organisation in Birmingham able to carry out long term after care in its field. With Haseley Hall established and continued help in the office from Anne Davies, Frank was able to cope with this himself. All ex patients were being seen every four months and some more frequently, valuable both in preventing relapses and also in giving an opportunity to teach parents how to avoid them.

Nevertheless, Frank, at 60, was beginning to feel the strain and suggested that the time had come when someone must be found to share the work and, eventually, take his place.

He was to stay with the Society for another six years, resigning at the end of March 1937. Haseley Hall had continued to run smoothly and the boarding out had also remained successful. In 1933, nine boys and nine girls were boarded out. Neville Chamberlain, the then Chancellor of the Exchequer had visited Haseley in 1934. All seemed blessed.

But even the numbers of girls at Haseley Hall and boarded out children combined could contribute no more than a small fraction of a solution to the problem of chorea and rheumatic disease in children. Others in Birmingham were also working on the problem but Frank continued to stress the value of the after care that the Society alone was able to offer and the opportunity it offered for the study of rheumatism and consequently the improvement of his methods of work. He describes what he does (1934):

"Every child who leaves Haseley or a farm is visited within a few weeks of returning home, and is seen constantly for the first two years, and at less frequent intervals afterwards, to assure ourselves that Doctor's orders are carried out, and necessary nourishment taken. Large quantities of cod liver oil and malt are distributed (either freely, or at a small charge) to make up for the deficiencies of diet. In any case of threatened relapse (though this is rare) the child returns to Haseley or a farm for a short period, and on returning home, careful watch is again kept.

Connected with the "After Care" we are able to do what we may call a little "salvage work" giving some small measure of happiness to the mothers by means of Convalescence, Dispensary Notes etc."

A couple of years later he adds:

"The After Care on which so much depends has been further developed. Through its reports to the Medical Officer of Health, Dr Newsholme, who is always willing to help us, we have been able to get some families removed from unhealthy houses to better ones, though, alas, there are still a number of urgent cases about which we are anxious. Weekly meetings of the After Care workers and the Staff are held at the Office, and all cases are discussed, especially those which have lately returned home. The interchange of opinion proves of the greatest help in dealing with those of a difficult nature. After Care covers a wide area. It deals with diet, additional nourishment in the form of Cod liver oil etc., bed time and hours of rest, suitability of employment, and conditions in the home. Where the children are attending school, visits are often paid to the teachers to ask for further information. Then there are other ways one can help besides the giving of advice or the spending of money – merely to listen to the difficulties, sometimes tragedies, of everyday life, will often bring some easement."

None of this is very different from the approach that Frank developed during his twenty five years with the Cripples Union. Its significance lies more in the way in which he saw it as differentiating his work from that of others in the field and therefore justifying the existence of his relatively small Society.

Also important was the way in which the Society was able to continue the whole treatment – at Haseley or on a farm plus after care – for as long as was deemed necessary and to learn the lessons that completed treatment could offer. He quotes the 1936 Report of the Schools Medical Officer for Birmingham, Dr G A Auden, who was also Honorary Consulting Physician for Haseley Hall:

"Another institution which provides for the treatment of rheumatic children is Haseley Hall, which has now been opened for five complete years under the Society for the Care of Invalid Children. Excluding five re-admissions for relapses, there have been 172 children dealt with, of which 107 can be reported as completed cases. These cases have been kept under continued review and the five years results are as under;-

95 doing well; 5 relapsed, of which 3 are now doing well and 2 still under treatment. 6 have proved unsatisfactory and 1 has been lost sight of.

The lesson to be learned from the experience thus gained is that institution treatment, if the best results are to be obtained, must be very prolonged in a large number of cases. Herein lies the great difficulty of the rheumatic child as a social problem. The number of cases so far exceeds the means for giving an adequately prolonged period of rest under truly hygienic surroundings that only a small fraction of the total number of cases which occur can obtain this essential. With the demand for beds for acute cases of illness the hospitals cannot retain these cases for the requisite length of time. Nor indeed is hospitalisation necessary for a large number of these children – what is wanted is more accommodation of the character of Baskerville and Haseley Hall where invalidism can be prevented by participation in a carefully regulated curriculum of educational supervision. Of the 107 Haseley Hall cases 92 were retained for twelve months or more. The results of the Invalid Children's Society's experience of boarding out children either in homes in the country or cottage hospitals point in the same direction – of 51 completed cases 30 stayed for twelve months or more..."

The next year, 1936-37 was to be Frank's last with the Society, the report for that year noting that he had resigned and that Mabel Baker had been appointed Secretary in his place from 31st March 1937.

Frank was, it is clear, doing good, much needed, work. There was no comparison with the end of his time with the Cripples' Union where, it could be argued, there was an inevitable qualitative change in the work to be done and the way of doing it. Why, then, did he decide to leave when he did?

It seems likely that he had become, whether he was conscious of it or not, bored with what he was doing. He had established a treatment method and had succeeded in opening a convalescent school. Although he had no great difficulty in raising funds to keep the work going there was no obvious possibility of increasing the scale of the work sufficiently to make serious inroads on the problem. Even what he had achieved was causing him to have to do a lot of routine administrative work that he disliked. His pocket diary records monthly meetings of several committees – General, Finance, Haseley Hall House Committee – which he was expected to attend as well as regular visitations that he felt obliged to carry out.

He says that he started the Society because, after leaving the Cripples' Union, he was free to tackle a problem that he had had to set aside during the early days of the Union. No doubt this was true but the circumstances in 1923 were different from those of 1900 or 1910. Others were, by now, working on the same problem, as he freely admitted and although he was able to make original contributions, most particularly in developing a family based approach to the illnesses of his patients and in his insistence on long after care, he may well have felt that he was no longer doing work that could not be done by others.

It has been suggested that, as with the Cripples' Union, he found himself at odds with his Committee. If so, there is no obvious sign of it in either the Annual Reports or the minutes of Committee meetings. He had, also, something new in mind and had already begun at least mental preparation for it. It is possible that his desire to change the direction of his work led first to conflict with his Committee and then to his decision to start afresh.

Whatever the reason for his going, Frank's departure seems to have had far reaching effects on the Society. The Committee reported the following year that 238 girls had been discharged as cured from Haseley Hall and it was able to continue with the school until 1941 when it was handed over to become one of the City of Birmingham's six open air schools. But, without Frank's continued and innovative fund raising, income started to fall away almost at once and the Society was soon forced to abandon boarding out. Frank was eventually to absorb what remained of the Society in his new venture.

1. Frank's birthplace, Market St, Wednesbury today.

2. Wednesbury Market Place today.   The bank building is on the left.

3. *A group of Cinderella Club children c.1895.*

4. *Children from the Cinderella Club c.1895.*

5. *Frank at 30, 1901.*

6. *Children at Chadwick End c.1905.*

7. A spinal carriage used by the Cripples Union c.1912.

8. *Evelyn Mathews at 40.*

9. *Frank in motor cycling gear c1920.*

10. *Original front of the Woodlands, now the Royal Orthopaedic Hospital.*

11. *The Forelands. Drawing from the brochure for the opening in 1921.*

12. Maple Road Bournville today.
No 47 is the second of the first pair of houses.

13. No 23 Laburnum Road, the office of the Birmingham Society for the
Care of Invalid and Nervous Children is to the left of this pair.

14. Hilda at 30, 1937.

15. Frank in 1943 at 47 Maple Road.

16. Aston Munslow with six children.
Back row: Rosa Price, Frank, Charles Burns c.1945.

17. Bodenham Manor in1947.

*18. Class Rooms,
Bodenham Manor School,
1969.*

*19. "The Laurels" Annexe,
Marden, 1969.*

HILDA PRICE

Frank's network of friends, many of whom he had made through his work, helped with fund raising and served on his committees and helped in the office. Groups such as the Ivy Fellowship and his Women's Guilds, made up of family members of patients, organised money raising activities.

But early in the history of the Invalid Children's Society he made an important new friend, Hilda Price, who he took on to work in the office at 47 Maple Road as shorthand typist, book keeper and general assistant.

She was born in 1907, the oldest of four daughters of George and Sarah Price. Her father had been a journeyman silversmith – a common occupation in Birmingham in the early 20th century – but by the time Hilda was at school he and Sarah were resident caretakers of a stove enamelling works in Green Street in the Deritend area of the city. As well as their ordinary caretaking responsibilities their job included making sure that the vats of enamel did not cool at night. Hilda told in later life how she and her sisters had been frightened by the glow of the furnaces in the factory yard.

George was not strong physically – he died at the beginning of 1933 - so it was Sarah who kept the family going. There was not much money and the house that came with the job was not particularly salubrious but the family seems to have been happy enough – a happiness marred when the third daughter, Nellie, died in a scarlet fever epidemic that saw all four girls admitted to the Isolation Hospital.

Hilda excelled at school, the Moseley Road Girls School, regularly winning prizes, but left at the minimum age, because her wages were needed. Her teacher, Miss A K Taylor, tried in vain to persuade Sarah to let Hilda remain as a pupil teacher – a lost opportunity that Hilda afterwards greatly regretted though she kept in touch with Miss Taylor for many years.

Instead she found a job as office girl at a small brass foundry owned by Harry Hall one of whose product lines was of objects of supposedly Egyptian appearance to be exported to Egypt for sale to tourists – again, a type of business not uncommon in Birmingham at the time. She did so well there that, after a few years, Harry Hall, who was a fair man and who remained a friend, advised her to move on, saying that his business would never be able to offer her a job that matched her talents. Hence she found herself employed, early in 1925, by the Birmingham Society for the Care of Invalid Children.

Her social life at this time was centred round the Digbeth Institute, and the Congregationalist Church and Girls Life Brigade associated with it, and her Night School studies, at the Central Evening Institute, which she had started in 1921 straight after leaving school. There she studied English, Commercial Arithmetic and Shorthand, winning the English prize, a copy of School for Scandal, in 1924. At Night School she had a circle of friends including, from 1924, Leslie Rees, her future husband. They had a long courtship and did not marry until 1930 when she was almost 23 years old.

Frank seems to have recognised quickly that he had found someone of exceptional talent for she soon shouldered greater responsibilities. By 1928, within three years of starting with the Society and aged only 21, she was named in the Annual Report as Assistant Secretary. As was the custom of the time she resigned, when she married, to become a full time housewife though there could not have been all that much for a childless young woman to do at home and the money from her job, had she kept it, would have been more than welcome: Leslie's job as a clerk with the Birmingham Corporation, though safe, did not pay much. Very soon she took up her education again, this time with the Workers' Educational Association, where she studied literature under and built up a long term friendship with her tutor Mrs F M McNeille, headmistress of a Girls School in the city.

As well as seeing her talent Frank took a very considerable personal liking to her and got into the way of writing long letters. About 60 of his letters to her have survived – one of her skills was the ability to read his writing and, fortunately, she transcribed a few. None of her replies seems to have been kept. At first Frank's letters were sent from his holidays in Wales, including his annual month's camping holiday with Evelyn, but after Hilda resigned they came, often enough, from his home in Bournville.

The first was written on 1st April 1926 and seems to be in reply to something from her, perhaps a draft for an Annual Report:

"Bodawen, Llanystumdwy, Criccieth, North Wales

Dear Hilda

Hurray it is indeed!!! There's no doubt that we are the people to run a charity – we can do it!!

I feel that tho' I have told you many times how much I appreciate your work for the Society and the help you give to me personally that I should at the close of our first year's work put the very sincere thanks and the warm appreciation I have for you on paper, it makes it more tangible somehow and a letter from a friend (and you and I have grown to be friends) is always a nice thing to have is it not? It is so nice to feel that I can say "Well done" and say it, as I have several times, without turning your head. You never take liberties as a result of it and unless I am mistaken you never will. You've made the work ten times easier and twenty times more interesting and we are both going to put our backs into it ((for)) the next twelve months and make it better and make up our minds not to rest until we have a proper Home of our own instead of looking all over the country and doing only second rate work, well worth doing as it is.

We were here by 6 o'clock but I did not enjoy the journey. I am too tired and it was very wet and misty after we left Llangollen. But we had a lovely walk today and things are better. I hope you'll have a nice Easter and not knock yourself out with too much tennis!

By the way should you start making the Balance Sheet before I get home I think Miss Holden's £145 should come in and I fancy it should go in on both sides as being transferred to a building fund...

I hope you will hear from the H((oliday)) F((ellowship)) soon and I am very anxious to know if you are in time. I...want you to get this experience.

Believe me to be yours affectionately

Frank Mathews.

The second, written about four months later from a camp site near Portmadoc, starts off in businesslike fashion but goes on to refer to the proposed stay with the Holiday Fellowship:

Dear Hilda

We have a lovely site here, almost perfect, and I don't want to come home any more or at any rate not till after the cold weather comes, tho' the weather is unsettled.

First will you ask Miss West to send us our gas account to pay. Will you ring up Mr Dutton and tell him I have not heard anything whatever of the second lot of income tax money (from Holden and Sons). I think we will leave the envelopes for Annual Meeting till I return. I'm not sure that I shan't send a letter instead of cards....Write Mrs Tomlinson.. and ask if she has moved yet and if she does move is she wishful to take children when I have some more....

What about the accounts. I expect you'll leave instructions about paying them. Tho' I'm absolutely certain its not necessary for me to bother about anything: it will all be straight.

I hope you'll have a topping holiday and enjoy it to the utmost. There will be a huge crowd at Conway – there are 98 there this week. Mind you don't bother yourselves with 'Guardian Angels' and such like. Let them go to the D****l or give them the slip if they wont. If your room the first week is not what you like look out for Miss Grey and sort of hint what you want and you'll get it. She is a great admirer of mine. Miss Schelling is very friendly too.

Yours affectionately

Frank Mathews

No ink left" – the letter is in pencil.

The next letter is undated. The reference to Hilda's 20th birthday suggests November 1927 but the relation of the content to one written in December 1926 shows that it must have been written in November 1926, only about three months after the last:

"With the Holiday Fellowship ((probably at Conway)) Friday evening

Dear Hilda

….I am very much afraid that I may have missed your birthday. I hope I haven't but anyway we'll make this a birthday letter and I'll tell you how very much I enjoy working with you and how much I like such letters as the one you sent me today. They are so natural and full of your friendship for me. I am very proud of your affection for me and very grateful to you for it. I often find myself wishing you had been a daughter of mine and planning what I would have done for and about you had you been. I would like to feel that our friendship is going to grow and develop till we know each other thoroughly.

For a long time I have been seeking an opportunity of discussing my philosophy of life with you as I feel I want you to understand the motives which make up my life (that's badly put but you will perhaps understand what I mean), I want you to want to know why I am a Socialist and why I do not hold the same religious beliefs as most other people, not so much because I want to convert you (I should like to convert you to Socialism – in religious matters I don't want to at all because I don't think in one sense they matter) but because Friendship means a perfect understanding and I don't like you being as I think you are, a little too cocksure of things you've not studied, you make me feel as if I had hit my head against a wall.

I should not feel that if I did not like you. I should not bother if I did not like you very much, but I get so much more from you than from any other friend that I have made that it is like that when you can't follow my thought.

I'm not in any way finding fault. I am really letting all reserve go and talking to you as if you really belonged to me. I wonder will this be your 20th birthday. I hope it is only that for I don't want to think of you getting old enough to leave me yet. Tell me what I should give you for your birthday when I get back. Tell me without my having to ask you I shall like that so much. But you'll think me a sentimental old Poodle if I say any more so that's that. Go slow on the toffee and the work after hours or you'll get tired and stale.

I've just been to Trefriw and Crafnant and wish you could have seen it with the Autumn colour. All over it are the beech woods a gorgeous yellow and oaks golden brown….I've only seen it once before…after a severe illness but is was a cold grey February day and I could not appreciate it as I did today. I do so want to feel that you've been on a real mountain top not with or in a crowd. Beautiful as these lakes are they do not move one as mountains do, though they are undoubtedly the next best thing. One aspires to the Divine on a beautiful mountain as nowhere else…

I'm delighted you like 'Night School' (though that's not a dignified description of it) and was more than pleased when you told me you had decided to go. When you've finished your technical education I am very anxious you should take up the History of the English people, Economic and Industrial History. It will make life so much more interesting and will give you the breadth of thought which is all you need to set you on the road to complete your Education. I can assure you that it is not in the least dull. It is as fascinating and surprising as any novel….

Well I shall get pen paralysis if I write any more. Letter writing is not my forte how I wish it were. I should like to be able to say everything I want to on paper but never can, or very rarely. As a rule to ((pick up)) a pen with me is to lose all thought of anything I want to say and to say it very badly as I expect I have in this letter but anyway however badly I have expressed myself I feel sure that the very warm affection I have for you must have come through the poverty of the expression of it. Accept my thanks my dear for all the help and sympathy you give me and believe me to be your very affectionate friend

Frank Mathews

I am afraid this is very difficult to read and very badly expressed and repeats itself but dare not try to rewrite it."

This letter is much more personal than the first two expressing, as it does feelings that are more appropriate to a familial context than to a working relationship, especially one so relatively new. It also, obviously represents a step in their relationship that was important to him.

The way the letter was put on paper, straight from the heart, with less attention than he customarily paid to grammar and punctuation, with handwriting even more hurried, if anything, than usual and with crossings out, is reminiscent of the manuscript of the most passionately felt of his sermons of thirty years before – 'Crippled Bairns'. It seems almost as though he had decided to gamble on entering into a deeper relationship with Hilda and was nervous about the outcome

Frank wrote again a few weeks later from his New Year holiday referring, apparently, to her reply:

"Trem-y-Don, Llwyngwril, 30 December 1926

Dear Hilda

Yes it was a very nice letter and I was not disappointed with it....

I am glad you had a really nice Christmas. I don't make much of

Christmas but I did enjoy seeing my 'nieces' ((Arthur's daughters)) at Stalybridge very much and I do look forward to the long quiet days here very much. You can have no idea of the beauty of a mountain country unless you have seen it in the Winter and I had a gloriously beautiful ride yesterday from Llangollen to here. At Bala the sun was shining on the lake with the mountains half shrouded in golden mists. Today I have been up in the hills all day (seeing) the mists and colours of the trees and wishing you were here with me so that I might answer your letter verbally instead of by letter.

Its so difficult for me to write about the things I feel most ((strongly)) about but I will try. I wonder why you do not think of going to the GLB ((Girls Life Brigade)) again next year, it seems a pity not to. The country around Nevin is very different to Llanfairfechan but it is beautiful in its way and there are some beautiful mountains overshadowing it – the 'Rivals'.

I can quite understand your not liking a Camp of 140. I do not think that either for boys or girls that big Camps are so good. There must be a loss of personal relations to some extent – they are somewhat watered down by large numbers. I don't believe in big things (of that sort) in any kind of work.

It is good that we both enjoy and appreciate working together, you may be perfectly sure that you get no more joy out of it than I do and we shall both get even more when you can put your reserve aside and talk to me freely. I do hope as time goes on you will succeed in doing this for my sake and still more for yours, as a reserve of this sort is a great hindrance all through life and may be a terrible danger to the success of marriage later. It is one of the greatest dangers to the success of married life and I expect and hope that you know Leslie so well already that it is already broken down, if it ever existed between you. Believe me it often prevents one discussing things of vital importance.

I realise fully the importance of a personal and friendly relationship in any work, and in work such as ours it is absolutely essential and if you will look back you will realise that right from the very first I set out to make our relationship one of friendship and complete understanding because I believe that good work can only be done when this is the basis.

As to 'taking interest in any little thing you do', I have grown to like you so much (as I told you in my last letter) that I almost wish you had been a child of my own. What a lot of jolly things we would have done together. When one loves anything…becomes a matter of interest so that it is merely a proof and a natural sequence of my affection for you that I should be interested in all your doings and all your thoughts (in reason) tho' the last thing I would like to do is pry into your affairs. I think it is our mutual affection for each other that makes me wish and long that you should be interested in the two things in which my whole life and thoughts are based. My religion and my belief in Socialism – both came to me together almost as a revelation. I am going to try and put them in this letter if I can but it is not too easy.

In one way you make me ashamed of myself, rather deeply ashamed. You say I almost seem to ridicule your Sunday school teaching. If I have done so I am very sorry and much ashamed, but I do not like Sunday schools as I consider them narrow and wrongly based. Children and adults are taught in them that there is only one true religion and that is Christianity, and I believe that there are many Religions and all are true. I have never had the opportunity or the ability to study Religion. (There is a science called the Study of Comparative Religions). But I do know there are several quite as beautiful as Christianity.

Confucianism, several of the Indian Religions and, (for me) above all Bhuddism which I love because it does not allow of taking of life at all. War which is the most horrible menace which exists today would be impossible were we all Bhuddists. I believe that no Bhuddist Nation has ever gone to War and it has more adherents than any other religion in the world. It has too, the doctrine of Reincarnation which makes one realise that the whole purpose of life here and hereafter and here again.

Until I heard of this I found the whole of life a muddle and an unhappy muddle too. By it all the anomalies are explained and one realises that there is no such thing as Sin. There is only experience and there is therefore no punishment in the hereafter, only the general attainment of Love and Freedom from Striving.

If you will think a little you will find that there is not a single 'sin' or there is no suffering in life which cannot be traced to selfishness – going to church is no service to God at all (as I see it) prayer is of no value to God, though it may be and more often than not is a help to pray. To me the only true prayer to God is one's acts . What we do for God and Humanity are our prayers, nothing else matters. Though as I said, prayer may help us, but set religions in places of Worship are so often, more often than not, anodynes which still our consciences rather than arouse them.

I admit that there are a good many people whose feelings must have some set form of religion to help them, but I would alter convictions so that they may be set for the highest religion of humanity. That there are so many religions, to me merely means that God so made them or allowed them, as so many pathways by which he may be reached by those of us who seek Him, and he having made all, there cannot be one true one and many false ones. To me it seems absurd that we who have merely finite minds should attempt to define the infinite.

You may fairly say to me "you preach self-sacrifice, you practise very poorly", I know too well I do and that leads me on to my other belief, that it is possible to so arrange Society that Health, Happiness, Education, Freedom and Love can be Birthrights of any one. I do not think for one moment that this can be achieved in 10 or 20 years although I have seen it come a good deal nearer than I had hoped in 33 years.

I think it will take another 100 or 150 years and that by the time Socialism arrives people will be dissatisfied and ((will wish to be?)) even nearer the divine than that. Then we shall go 'Forward through Law to lawless righteousness'.

As things are in England today for nearly seven eighths of the people a healthy life is impossible, for many a life free from sin is almost impossible, for some a life of sin is preordained by the circumstances in which they were born and the life of all of us is based on a system which makes most of us struggle for a living while a few of us live lives of comfort. One eighth of us have half the wealth of the country at the expense of the misery and unhealthiness of the remaining seven eighths. In the 'well to do' classes illness is more often than not an unpleasant incident, to the working classes it is a tragedy....

The whole of our present system is based on Profit for the few at the expense of the suffering of the many. Those of us who are Socialists believe, I would rather say know, that a system can be evolved which would be based on the good of the whole nation rather than on the good of a few at the expense of the many. Tho' in saying this I am not speaking quite as I think for I do believe that those who do hold the wealth of the country do not for the most part benefit. The wealth accumulates in quantities greater than they can use, harms them morally and spiritually even more than poverty harms it victims.

There now dear Hilda you have my Basis of life probably very poorly put but I told you before expressing my thoughts on paper. If ever you and Leslie can see the utter hideousness of the streets all around you and realise that what you and I are trying to do is almost wasted effort and what might happen if everyone of us were to realise the horror of modern life and set to work to right it. Then you would soon become, like myself, a Socialist before anything else. Believe me there is no hope for us to become religious in the best sense until we have a Social life based on the good of all.

I am not sure that I can quote accurately some verses of Whittier which seem to sum up all I would say but you can look him up some time and correct this.

'Oh, Brother Man fold to thy heart thy Brother
Where Pity dwells, the peace of God is there,
To Worship rightly is to Love each other'
Each smile a hymn, each kindly deed a prayer.....'

There Hilda dear, what about 'pen paralysis' I've not written a letter as long as this for 20 years (and a good thing too I hear you murmur)

With warmest wishes for a Happy year for you … and that we may go on working happily for many years yet (don't repeat this wish to Leslie)

I am, always yours affectionately,

Frank Mathews."

This seems to be the most complete statement that Frank ever made of his religious and political beliefs but it would not have surprised anyone who had followed his activities over the previous thirty years. His religious position reflects the Unitarian view on the potential validity of all beliefs and also his early interest in spiritualism. His preference for Bhuddism may owe something to the influence of Edward Carpenter.

His socialism too bears the marks of his reading, particularly of the early Fabian Tracts, and of his membership of the Labour Church. He would not be himself if he were not interested in the hard facts about the injustices that socialism would right or the practicalities of achieving that end but it is clear that he follows William Morris, and the mystic socialism of Carpenter, rather than the more pragmatic ideas adopted by the Labour Party of his later years.

Perhaps the most interesting point in the letter is his throw away remark about the work he was, and had been, doing being "almost wasted effort" as if he felt that his life might have been better spent reforming the world's institutions rather than ameliorating the effects of the ones in place. This was a theme he was to come back to, but whatever his thoughts, it is abundantly clear that he always felt compelled to do something practical to remedy the conditions he found. It is clear too that he was doing what he was best fitted to do. As well has having no interest in practical politics he had a temperament – impatiently energetic and intolerant of consensus compromise – that would have made him completely unsuitable for it.

Hilda may or may not have noticed the oddness of her receiving letters of such passionate intensity from an educated man thirty odd years her senior. If she did, she may have assumed that they derived from fatherly feelings toward her. But, whatever her reaction, it is clear that she either did not wish or did not know how to reply, much to his dismay.

Four months later, at Easter 1927, he writes from Llwyngwril:

> "I want to begin my letter by repeating what I have said to you so often, that you (and your affection for me) are more to me than anyone (apart from Mrs Mathews) I have ever had to do with, that your welfare and happiness are somehow bound up in mine, in return for what I give you in love and sympathy you give me a great deal, a very great deal, and if one thanked those who loved one for their love and affection I should thank you, but where there is true love thanks are unnecessary on either side. Love takes the place of thanks, does not need it.

> The weak side of your affection for me is its lack of understanding, your affection is a little too sentimental, all this is ((leading)) to an affectionate grumble that you should have left a letter of mine unanswered for 4 months, …you don't realise all the things I may have been thinking all that time and that I may possibly have been hurt by what I know was not really neglect but was felt like it.

> Your greatest weakness is the weakness of all ardent young people. It is that you see your own position much more clearly than the other person's, in a word you have to clear yourself of unconscious egotism. I can't tell what you are thinking and, as I have said to you so often I am afraid of forcing myself and my ideas on you. Could you not put just one hour a month apart to telling me where you are mentally….if moods stand in the way break this down, you will find you can if you will force yourself to do so…..

> I think the service that you and I are giving is all right as far as it goes but it's second rate service. It is merely palliative work, it leaves untouched the appalling problem of Poverty and its prevention and cure. I don't suppose there is any possibility of it

happening, but if ever, when you knew more, you told me that what we are doing is not good enough and that you must give it up and give all your interest to the real salvation of humanity it would be the happiest day of my life.

I think, in the mean time we can go on working together doing the work we are doing in the broadest possible terms but there is no hope for the wider religious thought that you and I are so interested in until people are free from the burden , misery and degradation of poverty....

Further, I would say, don't judge people by their ability to adopt the new religious ideas I have opened out to you. The fact that there can be so many different views is probably because there are so many different kinds of people on earth, so many people in different stages of development. As each civilisation develops so will real religious thought and it seems to me ((to be)) another argument for Socialism, that as it develops so will people be able to become religiously emancipated.

Tell me when you can how you stand mentally towards Socialism. I have not the haziest idea....Have you reached the point where you realise that no true Religion is possible while crime, poverty, war and unnecessary suffering exist, that none of us is free while one of us remains in slavery of either mind or body...

There my dear child, there's another long screed from FM...One more minute. You may wonder why I am in such a hurry. I feel I've only this next year or so before you marry. After this we are bound to be more out of touch and I need to lay the foundations before then.

Always your affectionately, . . ."

The next letter, dated 14 July 1927, came from his holiday camp site in North Wales. The first page deals with the business of the Society. It is clear that he was still taking at least some of his work with him:

"Dear Hilda

The papers and letter you sent suffered severely in a … torrent this morning when the river burst its banks…we thought we had a flood the night before but it was a mere dribble to what we had this morning. As I had a bad night and a busy morning I may not be as intelligent as I would like.

Say to Mr Lees that that for the moment I cannot do anything for the boy. I will try in the late Autumn but I think it may be advisable to send ((him)) away for three weeks before the winter as a safeguard. (Send him to Mrs Dunn when she has a vacancy.)…I've written to the Broke people God Bless 'Em and am thankful that the letter along with two more survived the flood.

I'll tell you what made me unhappy if you will promise me you won't think I'm blaming you. You haven't answered my letter at Christmas (not really). At Easter when I asked you to let me know how you got on I had nothing and when I wrote your reply upset me a little. When you went to Kenilworth I asked for a p.c. You wrote to everyone else and never sent me a card to say how you were. Naturally I was wondering what I could have done to hurt or annoy you. No, I have not more in common with Miss Davies than with you, not nearly so much really. I never saw Miss Davies for more than a minute or two before she came to the office. I like her very much and am grateful to her for her enthusiastic help.

Don't let this idea grow or it might easily grow and grow to prevent a friendship; there is nothing whatever in it.

The difference if any was due to my misunderstanding your note at Easter and nothing else and it was not, I repeat, that I blamed you but could not think of a cause. Let it go, say no more about it and start afresh.

As to my being more reserved than you, this is a mistake. I am an unusually outspoken person with my friends but….I know I must not force my personality and ideas on you and that holds me back a good deal. If you can break down your reserve you'll find I have none, reserves between friends are the most fatal of things, friendship with them is impossible.

I feel too that most of your friends are diametrically opposed to me in most things and that probably you don't want me putting in your mind views that may upset them. I am a very new friend compared with them.

Naturally as my friend with unusual abilities I want to see you use them as I think it's the greatest scourge of humanity, and you seem to me to hold back all the time and I don't understand why unless the previous paragraph of my letter accounts for it.

There now my dear I've done, but don't on any account read into this note anything I've not written. Writing it I've put aside all ((reserve)) entirely and written to you as if I were 20! If only I were I'd give you no peace until we had talked out my ideas and your objections to them.

Believe me to be yours affectionately, Frank Mathews."

This correspondence obviously caused Frank a deal of anguish. Hilda too would have been uncomfortable and confused, but, clearly, it did not spill over into their working relationship in a way that she did not feel able to handle.

The letters, and whatever else passed between them seem to have cleared the air to some extent. Six months later, at New Year 1928, he is writing from Llwyngwril in a more measured way:

"Dear Hilda

I have just put down a most exciting and fascinating book to write to you – so we are quits, are we not.

I was so pleased to get your letter, I always prize them and look forward to them. I expect its almost impossible for one so much younger to realise the pleasure you can give by a letter or a friendly chat now and again. You look on we 'older ones' as people of a different class altogether, you do it even if it is unconsciously. A very happy New Year to you and so many thanks for the cushion which I value very much.

I dearly love presents but am always afraid of people getting into the habit of giving them so that they become mechanical and are given because they always have been. A present given after a friendship is dead is as bad as throwing a stone at one, and if presents are given at odd times one knows that they are not just Christmas and birthday presents but are real tokens of affection. My little presents to you are different, it's a great privilege when you young people let us older ones enter into your lives and…the privilege is greater when one has no children of ones own. Not that I've ever wanted children of my own, I've always been afraid of their growing up and being different from what one would wish ones children to be. Many thanks my dear for your love and help – may it grow and last for my lifetime.

I wonder why it is such an immense pleasure to share ones ideas with others. I am trying to put it into worlds and cannot, except that the ideas we have grown to share are those which govern all my life and there are so few people who do share them … I know of course why I want you to become a Socialist but why I'd like you to come with me into the wider religious world of thought I don't quite know…."

And from his summer holiday, in July:

"Cae Du, 4 July 1928,

Dear Hilda

Its raining again and has been since six last night so, as my mind is more rested I am going to try to write to you, tho' whether I am clear enough to say all I want to I'm not sure. Anyway, make allowance for a mind still somewhat fagged.

We seem to get no chance to talk at home ever and if, now and again you sort of drop things at me as if you were in constant mental touch with me as if I knew all that went on in your mind, you don't realise that, tho' you have dropped a great deal of your reserve with me there is still a lot left making a mind I can't see through. Anyway we know each other a lot better than we did this time last year but we've a long way to go for a complete understanding of each other's mental standpoint.

I am constantly wondering whether I have not done more harm than good in disturbing your religious beliefs, have taken away one that was to you, definite and left you with another that does not give you the same clear strength. Tell me if I have. To me the change from one to another brought with it a greater one and, I always think, a more useful one.

I feel that those of us who have given up the old ideas of religion should find in its place the helping of humanity out of the bog of poverty and misery in which it is at present – you asked me one day not long ago, did I want you to join a Socialist group (at least I thought that was what you meant). I do when the urge within yourself is so great that you have to. I don't want you to do it to please me, it would not last when my personal contact with you waned as, alas, it must do in a year or two (the alas is for me not for you my dear). What I want to do is for you to be so convinced that the conviction itself will make you do it. I want to feel that if you have children they will be brought up to the real responsibility of man for man's sufferings and for man's happiness.

I know you love me and I you very dearly but love is a thing by itself, it doesn't involve doing things for love's sake. There is no compulsion in it, not even love's compulsion.

Don't feel because you and I are so fond of each other that you ((have)) to do as I do or think as I do. That would be mere ointment. If one can do it without being morbid (and you can) one should, every now and again, take stock of ones ideas and see if one's lives fit in with them.

I am not saying for a moment that you cannot do this. I am not preaching to you (not wilfully anyway) but we are in some way so shut off from each other that I don't know what your mental processes are or where they are leading you.

I am sure you know that the last thing I would do would be to impose my mind on yours, or my soul were such a thing possible but I do want to awaken and strengthen that fine mind and soul of yours and still there is so much risk of its getting into a rut and being contented with it. At least, in my lack of knowledge of the direction of your thought that is what I feel….

Tell me about yourself for all of you interests me…"

However, despite the quieter terms he does not seem to be able to achieve the meeting of minds that he desires and by early 1929, when he was 58 and Hilda 21, he gives voice to his frustration:

"With the Holiday Fellowship (Conway) 1 April 1929

Dear Hilda

I feel I should begin by apologising for interfering with you so often but its largely your fault. I have had so many girls working with me during the last 30 years and of all of them you are the only one I thought it worthwhile to tell my thoughts to or to try to influence in any way and yet I seem to have failed so badly. I suppose I have used the wrong methods or put my case badly or not made what I value as clear to you as it is to me.

But you took the talking ((to)) I gave you so nicely some weeks ago that I want to try to have one more try to get to understand you and for you to understand me. Will you begin by taking my assurance that I am fond of you, very fond of you, (I often wish I were 27). Were I not I should, as I have told you before, shrug my shoulders and leave off attempting to influence you.

After this explanation I am go((ing)) on to say the things I have to say.

The longer you are with me the more of an enigma you are to me. I can only account for the inconsistencies by thinking you must have a clear and definite purpose in life.

When you came to me you were active at Digbeth taking a useful part in the Brigade, helping in several other useful things, going to classes and to evening classes for French and English,. Indeed I thought you were working beyond your strength.

You gave up all Brigade work and all Digbeth work except Sunday School. You went on with French and English, (I don't mention the business classes, I don't think this important).

Then you gave up French and English classes, thus, as it seemed to me, wasting all the time and money you had spent as regards the French (for half learned French is useless) and most of the money and time you have spent on English seem to me to be wasted. You took up singing at which you can never hope to excel for you have no real love of music, at least I have failed to find it and I have tried on several occasions to see if you had without asking you a direct question.

You gaily adopt the new religion as I posited it to you but I cannot see that you have adopted any of its implications. Ask yourself what difference the change has made in your life, has it been good or bad or neutral? You say you miss the help you got from Digbeth and yet you make no attempt to find anything to take its place.

You undertook to do some voluntary work for me and never touched it. I could understand that you may have found it impossible. I could not understand your not telling me so. And yet, whenever I tell you to do a thing, even out of office hours it is done promptly and done well….

Again, I was puzzled and hurt all through the summer by your refusal to answer my last letter. I am still at a loss utterly. I cannot think of any unkind act that I have done. I have never since I have known you had an unkind thought. I've none now and yet you could not, or would not, do that which would have saved some pain and disappointment….

All these things seem to me to be caused by having no plan in life at all, by living in the moment only, which is contrary to all I have tried to teach you. The whole of ones life, both personal and business must centre around ones creed or both the creed and the life are wasted.

Analyse your life for the last six months and this will tell yourself how much of it apart from the office was any use to other people and to the bringing out of your character. What have you accomplished?

I expect an answer to this letter though not by return of post by any manner of means. I do not want you to write and agree with all I have said, probably I may have said some things that are incorrect. I have put my case against you as strongly as I know how, have possibly exaggerated it – I think I have.

You probably see all sorts of difficulties that I know nothing about but I don't know them because you never tell me of them. I want you to write and defend yourself, not just tell me 'you are right'. There must be some explanations you can give. I have never asked anything in return for the ((regard)) I have shown you and you have given me little that I cared for in return so far. I am asking if you have, as I believe you have, really any warm affection for me. Let me know where you stand, what your purpose in life is, what your religion is, what your attitude to social questions is.

Or write and tell me you would rather not answer this letter. Quite likely you would rather not do so. I may be disappointed but you know me too well to think for a moment that I would let you see the slightest difference in my treatment of you.

In closing this letter I want to reiterate that I am very fond of you for if I were not it would not have been written but of late I have begun to despair at times ((and)) to wonder if you have more than a sentimental attachment to me.

I am dear Hilda, Always yours affectionately,"

This is the last dated letter he wrote to Hilda before her marriage in September of the following year but there is one short undated one that seems to bring this phase of their correspondence to a close. It is written on the same headed paper as the one before and so may have been written either a few days later in the same holiday or during a later one in the autumn. Whatever she wrote to him, or several months of silence, must have given him some pause for thought:

"I was very pleased to get a little personal note from you again, as you know it was five months since you'd written one. Anyway, I am so glad as it leaves me free to talk to you again (I had come to the conclusion that you didn't want me to do so) and I have a lot I want to say to you if only I can manage to get it out!

I think your difficulty is that once you leave the office you leave all method behind you and you let your mind become unmethodical, forgetting what construction those who love you, or at any (rate) one who loves you, may put on your silence.

I think I must alter my methods but I don't want to write. I don't yet feel sure enough of not 'putting my foot in it' again so will wait until we can have an uninterrupted talk. Anyway, dear, believe me when I say I do love you and that even your long silence has not affected this but has left me puzzled and, at times, a little hurt.

I am horrified to think of you and Les doing the wireless in a cold house and hope you are neither of you the worse for it. I wish I had known, I would have told them to light the stove. Anyway, with my warmest thanks,

With love, yours affectionately"

* * *

What is to be made of this correspondence?

Even without Hilda's side of it, such as it was, it is pretty clear that she was a reluctant participant. Nor is this surprising.

She held Frank in great esteem, not that she would ever have thought of him as Frank – he was Mr Mathews to her till the day he died. She would have known from his presence, which was very strong, and from the attitudes of those around him that he was a formidable person and she would have known, in outline at least, of the great things that he had already achieved. She would have been flattered, and embarrassed, by the way he addressed her.

But she would have known little about the subjects he was so anxious to discuss with her.

The ideas behind Frank's socialism, which advocated a society radically reformed toward fairness without any very clear suggestion of how it might be brought about or what the situation might be when it had been achieved, might have reached her through the teachings of her church. Indeed, they did not seem to have given her any difficulty. She, and her husband, joined the Labour Party in their mid thirties and remained active in it, in a very practical way, for the rest of their lives.

Her family had little, if any, interest in politics and, though the Labour Party had gained in parliamentary strength to the point where it could form a minority national government it did not become strong in Birmingham until after the second world war. If her parents voted in the 1920's they might well have voted Liberal. Socialism, as advocated by Frank, would have been a subject for discussion among intellectuals. She might well have felt, at the time when Frank was trying to convert her, that there was little that she could usefully say about it.

She would probably have known nobody who was not either Christian or Jewish and was most unlikely to have known anything about the teachings of other faiths – or, indeed about the existence of some of those mentioned by Frank. She had been brought up in the Congregationalist church, where she found much of her social life, and was thoroughly familiar with the better known parts of Old and New Testament history. But her own Christianity came more from acceptance than conviction and, though she never ceased to guide her life with the Christian ethic, or something close to it, her religion soon ceased to be uppermost in her mind. She was married in the Congregationalist church at Digbeth but became, and remained until her mid thirties a nominal adherent of the Church of England: thereafter, religious questions seem not to have troubled her.

So she would have found Frank's ideas about religion novel but not necessarily shocking nor even as vitally interesting as he did.

But the point that Frank missed was that she was occupied with a radical change that was coming about in her personal life. Hitherto it had been based on her family and, particularly on her two younger sisters with whom she shared her enthusiasm for the activities associated with the Digbeth Institute. Now she had found a new focal point for her social life, her night school where she had formed a group of friends and had met the young man she would marry. Her adjustment to that and her preoccupation with getting to know him did not leave much space in her life for philosophical discussion with Frank.

It would be possible to get into all sorts of speculation about what the sequence of letters tells us about Frank's character and state of mind. Nowadays, and perhaps then, they would have been considered inappropriate, to say the least, coming, as they did from an older man in a position of authority and being directed at a young female employee. No doubt Frank would have been horrified at any suggestion that the letters could be viewed in this way.

It would hardly have been surprising if Hilda, unable to cope with his pressure, had simply gone away. Jobs were hard to find but she was by now well qualified and she would probably have found something else without too much difficulty. Why did Frank take the risk?

Perhaps he judged – and he had by this time reason to be confident in his judgment of people – that she would be able to put aside the master – servant aspect of their relationship and deal with him as an equal over things not connected with her work. If so, he was right in the limited sense that she does not appear to have been particularly frightened of him but he seems to have greatly underestimated the effect of the differences in their culture and experience on her ability to engage in any kind of argument and greatly overestimated the importance that she would put on the exchange in the context of her own expanding life.

It is more interesting, however, to speculate about why he should want to educate her into his beliefs.

His reasons were, no doubt, based on his perception that she was a young person of fine mind and character, well worth the trouble of educating. But why not try to educate her in cultural matters, in which her education was deficient and which she would later, and partly under his tutelage, study with enthusiasm. That he should chose religion and politics, the subjects that he judged central to his own existence must surely suggest that he saw his relationship with her in close personal rather than pedagogic terms.

In his letters he more than once refers to the idea that she might have been a surrogate daughter. The age difference was right and he was childless and it is tempting to see things only in this light. He says that he is not sorry to have no children of his own as they might have disappointed him if he had, the implication being that Hilda, under his tuition, would not be subject to such a failing. It is odd that someone as familiar with the work of Bernard Shaw as Frank certainly was would fail to spot such an implication.

He may have seen her consciously or, more likely not, as a surrogate daughter in another sense. As he approached his sixtieth birthday the question of who was to succeed him in his work became increasingly urgent for him and he may have considered her for this role and felt that a common view on life philosophy was an important attribute for a suitable person. If so, he would have been right, as it eventually turned out, to consider her but wrong to think that the details of the common view mattered very much.

But there may have been more to it than that. In one of his later letters he wishes that he were thirty years younger and it is tempting to wonder if, at the back of his heart he feels himself to be in a way a suitor, laying before her his most precious possessions. It is unimaginable that the thought crossed his conscious mind – he would have backed off immediately if it had – but it is striking that the tone and content of his letters to her changed radically as soon as she was married.

Be all that as it may, it is clear that either none of this communicated itself to Evelyn or, if she had any idea that such a correspondence existed, she played with the straightest of bats. The last letter to Hilda before her marriage was from Evelyn:

"Cae Du June 15th 1930

Dear Miss Price

It was quite all right about the letter – thanks for sending it on. I'm so glad that the WG ((Womens' Guild)) turned up in such force – I wonder how they have done with their share of the house to house collection – perhaps its too early to judge, yet. I shall be back in time to put my 'mite' to the sale.

This morning we received the enclosed (£2 notes) from my sister – Mrs Carl Heath, White Wings, Onslow, Nr Guildford, Surrey – a collection at the Friends Yearly Meeting. Will you please send a formal receipt made out as 'Collected at the Friends Yearly Meeting per Mrs Carl Heath. Mr Mathews would like it to go to the building fund.

Re Buckets: we find that although we soaked one and kept it filled in running water for 3 days it emptied itself in 20 mins! Can you write to the people from whom you bought them for us, and ask how to make them hold water? We are bringing them back, and should really like to change them as they are a different pattern to 'ours' – bigger and heavier.

On the whole the weather has been very good to us, and at the moment the sun shines gloriously and I am off for a bathe, having forwarded the dinner and tidied up the tent.

I hope your father and mother are having the same lovely sunshine and that the former is very much better and the latter feeling rested. No doubt you will be glad to see them back again, if only from a purely selfish point of view.

Greetings to all at the office, especially yourself, from,

Sincerely yours, Evelyn Mathews.

I write this with my new 'Herald' pen – I feel it improves my handwriting and hope the improvement extends to more valuable things as well!

If Evelyn was playing with a straight bat she was showing admirable judgement as events were to show.

TRANSITIONS

Hilda married Leslie Rees in September 1930 and, for a short time, seems to have been too busy to devote much time to Frank and his affairs. He was present at her wedding but he did not write to her until November the next year when he sent her a letter from the Holiday Fellowship at Conway.

The tone of this letter is completely different from those before she married. It is as though he has accepted that she has changed from being someone he must somehow train to conform to his values to being a friend and confidant who, though she is younger and less experienced, he treats as a social equal.

He starts off by apologising for the quality of his letter and goes on to say that he is sorry that he has not felt able to use his influence to help a friend of hers get a job at Haseley. He tells her of a journey he has had to make to Birmingham and back in the middle of his holiday giving details of the timing and remarking that it was "Not bad for 60".

The question of his age comes up several times in his letters over the next few years. He also refers repeatedly to his tiredness at the beginning of the frequent holidays that he feels obliged to take and it is clear that he was feeling the strain of the workload that he was undertaking.

The same sort of thing happened in the last years of his work for the Cripples' Union and it may, in both cases, have been an indication that he was not altogether happy with what he was doing. It would not have been so much that he didn't think that the right things were being done as that he found the day to day routine burdensome. This time he was almost ten years older and the pressures would have been harder to deal with.

By the summer of 1932 Hilda was expecting her first child and both Evelyn and Frank wrote early in July from their holiday to wish her well, Evelyn mentioning her pleasure that Hilda hoped to return to the Women's Guild in September. Frank gives an idea of his own mood:

> "…We've been here a fortnight now and I wish to goodness I was never going back (at least I almost do!) Nothing has suffered. Now we have got a bell tent all the excitement has gone out of camping tho' we can easily do without it. The weather has been glorious and I am very well. We've had one glorious walk and should have had two more but Mrs Mathews is so lazy here she won't walk…"

and then, on July 26th he wrote:

> "Thank the Lord that's over, we were beginning to wonder;
>
> Whether you had forgotten us,
> Whether things had gone wrong,
> Whether Antony had missed the celestial train or the stork had lost its way!
>
> That's my flippant way of referring to the birth of one who may remake the world. (God knows it needs it.) I hope he will and will bring you all, or nearly all, the happiness you hope for from him and for him, tho' I do not wish for too much happiness for him. Too much happiness means, as a rule, too little character.
>
> I'm not, as you know, not very fond of children, specially very little ones, they frighten me, but I'm very interested to watch the result of having them on their parents. Will you lose the world in Antony? I hope not entirely, indeed I hope you will find a new and stronger cause to try and right it for him and his generation. It's a rotten hole now.

But you're saying 'why the old man is sermonising, (which is a thing he likes doing to those he loves) so I'll shut up and send you and Leslie my love and congratulations.

I hope you'll take great care for the necessary time and you may be sure that as soon as the crowd of baby admirers has passed by, you'll let the baby disliker come along and see you. How soon are you receiving?

Yours very affectionately, Frank Mathews

PS Will you please get me 108v Ever Ready battery and tell the office people to send for and pay for it.

From that point on he started to write fairly frequently and it seems that she, with less to do and probably finding it easier to know what to say, replied.

In November he wrote:

"I so often plan to do things that don't come off, so I am anticipating your birthday next Sunday, for once, ((lest)) I should be prevented from coming to see you tho' I fully intend to do so. I am also sending you my present for your birthday and sending it with my…love and hoping you'll have a happy and useful life. I refrain from wishing you a long one: you may, like me, get somewhat tired about 50 or 60 and wish, like me, to see what is to follow it, if anything does and I think and hope that something does. I would…like to see what happens to our civilization and whether my hopes for it are true ones, tho' I don't want to remain in the world to see it…"

It comes as a bit of a shock, nowadays, that Frank should consider himself old at the age of 60, though it would not have been so surprising at the time. But his interest in his own and others mortality was to recur in his letters. Hilda's father died just after Christmas 1932 and Frank wrote a letter of condolence from his holiday at Llwyngwril:

"My love and sympathy to you and still more to your mother.

I don't quite know what to say to comfort you, I wish I were at home to talk to you. I'm so unorthodox about death that I am afraid of hurting those I would comfort. So I say that you should take comfort that if you have lost one you love, you have your baby to love, and the more I see of you the fonder I am of you, you are, as I have so often told you, more like a child of my own than just a friend and one must live in the love that others give us and that we give them in turn.

You may be feeling that your father never had much of a life and if one looks on a life on this plane as final it seems to have been a waste to some extent from his point of view. But if one believes (or almost believes) as I do that 'Life here is a life but just begun, a long race only entered on'…for ((death)) is merely a passing through a door with a line to sum up what we have gained and lost. I don't really believe any of us, not even the worst of us, can lose anything by our life on this plane there is all eternity to profit by our losses when we can see what they are and how we incurred them.

But I believe…that we choose…our lives, and choose them deliberately because we desire to gain some particular good quality or lose some bad one and to do this we must assume bodies which go through particular experiences…

But suppose I am wrong in my theory of Reincarnation…Death means annihilation: well what of it, one can't be unhappy when annihilated and one cannot suffer then…"

He wrote several more times during the first half of 1933, the next letter only a couple of weeks later on 16 January commiserating with her having to accommodate her in-laws and talking over a visit to see her and the baby, when he seems to have found the baby a hindrance to relaxed conversation. In May he wrote acknowledging a letter from her and describing a holiday to the Roman wall and the Lake District and in July from his holiday camp site:

"Cae Du, Towyn, July 7th 1933

Dear Hilda

What a nice long letter, I'm afraid I can't equal it, there is not much news. We had a glorious day on Cader yesterday… Mrs Mathews was with me. We did not get to the actual summit, only about ten minutes from it. But its not the summit (in mountains anyway) that counts. It's the whole surroundings and what the mountain says to one and it said many things to me. The loveliest was 'you're not quite done in, you shall see me a few more times' and I am so happy. How I should have tried to initiate you into the wonders of the mountains, there is nothing on earth like them, particularly on mountains one loves. But Mrs Mathews has developed a flat foot or a rheumatic foot or something and I'm wondering if we shall get up again.

I don't like you to feel out of it in any respect…Tell Gwen ((Hazelwood)) to let you have the monthly financial statements…there are usually some left after Finance Committee.

I have neglected your education in the matter of the Classics I'm afraid but I'm not good at literature at all but here ((is)) some sound advice:

Thackeray Esmond, The Virginians (a sort of continuation) and The Newcomes. Pendennis is not bad

Dickens Tale of Two Cities, Hard Times, David Copperfield, Our Mutual Friend, but I find that I should put down all Dickens tho' I always skip the melodrama., but The Old Curiosity Shop is all melodrama. I never read that again.

Jane Austen Emma and all Jane Austen. She is considered very good literature.

Mrs Gaskell All, tho' I think you know them.

Trollope All the Barchester Towers series…

Charles Read Never too late to mend, and The Cloister and the Hearth.

George Gissing All, tho' they are very miserable books but one can never leave them unfinished once begun

Thomas Hardy Tess of the D'Urbervilles and all his tho' he is too melodramatic for me

George Meredith Richard Feverel is the only one I can read, but I ought to be able to read any.

Henry James too is far beyond me but one ought to know him.

Lord Lytton …I am ashamed to say that I enjoy them all..

I think this list will keep you busy till Baby is weaned. If you still have time for more after that event I'll have another go…

Well, I'm not sure the baby is not crying so I'd better stop…"

He wrote again on 10th July, a picture postcard of Cader Idris, asking for a letter and then again on the 15th acknowledging it:

"What a pleasure it is to get your letter, what a pity you were not from twenty years or so sooner and then, by the time I 'popped it' you could have written a 'Life and Times of an Obscure Philanthropist'. You appear to be able to read them, which is more than most people can.

It's been very poor weather this last week, rain most days and dry nights, but I've never slept so well and never enjoyed an absolutely lazy holiday before. Alas, not a walk yet but I don't enjoy walking with other people (not even with Mrs Mathews) really now…I intensely enjoy walking alone but that's the very thing Mrs Mathews can't understand and it pains her that I want to, so I let it go. Our life together is so wonderful and (I think) unique that I can easily afford to give up that I love, and it is very good to give up things, I think.

Camping with anyone you are in complete sympathy ((with)) is an ideal holiday especially in a place almost all to oneself. It is very beautiful here today, a subdued sunlight and the whole of the bay in view from Bardsey to Harlech with great masses of clouds gathering over Snowdonia…..

There is a chance that we may do something about a successor during the coming year. Mrs Mathews' brother ((Bernard d. 1932)) left some shares in the firm which, if left in the firm (Holdens), would bring in a good income and thus I could afford to give up the honorarium and devote ((the money)) to paying a successor. But all is in the air and is in confidence between you and I. (Or me, what is it?)

I had a letter from Gwen just after she came back which interested me intensely. It seemed as if she had woken up or had begun to do so. I do hope so as there is, I am sure, much ability in her, tho' I don't agree with you entirely. I think the thing holding her back most is intellectual slovenliness and lack of wise self criticism. I told her so but she has not answered my letter yet. I hope I have not put my foot in it, just as she seemed to coming along as a possible Mathewsite!!

…As to influencing your boy, I think you should try all you can to do so, but I've seen such extraordinary results in parents and their children that I often wonder whether we really can do anything. But I am sure that we must try to do so but be prepared to be philosophical about the results and above all to keep our affection when we fail. I think that the inability to do this to a large extent is my greatest weakness. I would almost call it a 'sin' if I believed in sin. I cannot be out and out affectionate and loving to people unless I have a great deal, or at least something, in common. Mrs Mathews can be, I simply don't know how and yet I feel such a beast when I lose interest in young people who have grown up under my care….

We have both been reading D. H. Lawrence's Letters. Did you read any of his books? Did you read 'Sons and Lovers', its marvellously done, get it out of the library…I don't like the man after reading his letters, not at all, and I won't like 'Sons and Lovers' but I'll read it again when I get back…

I'm glad the holiday was a fair success, its good to get away from the daily round…now and again. I hope when the boy is older you'll take to camping. Perhaps by that time we shall be too old for it and you are assured of our outfit. Its very complete and very comfortable.

Well I expect this is as much as you can decipher and its all I have to say at the present so its au revoir with much love.

Yours always affectionately, Frank Mathews"

It appears that he may have been considering Gwen Hazelwood either as a possible successor or as someone he could rely on in the longer term. She was about the same age as Hilda but had been delicate as a child with some signs of heart disease. Quite how she had come under Frank's care is unclear – she stayed at Salway Farm, near Droitwich, for a considerable period around 1930 when she was in her early twenties but she was too old to have been treated as a child by his present Society – but she had made a good recovery, aided by an enjoyment of mountain walking.

She did not succeed him but she did stay with his Societies until she died in 1970. She became a friend of Hilda's and honorary aunt to her children.

The last letter of the year, written on September 9th and presumably in response to birthday greetings, came from Bournville:

"That's a relief. I have so very few great friends that I am reluctant to lose one and I hate hurting anybody tho' in my haste I sometimes do so.

You are quite mistaken, I love presents, above most things, I like them so much. Tho' I like to be certain they are spontaneous, that's why I discourage my friends from giving me one every year lest they get the habit and feel they have to go on giving me them when their affection has waned or partly waned. People seem to get tired of me after a time, I must be getting more of a bore as I get older. I hate the thought of it tho', not getting old but boring people.

If you must give me a book I have not 'The Way of All Flesh' but I don't know if there is a cheap edition. Please don't get it if there is not.

We had a perfect day at Haseley on Monday and both of us came home very happy.

Its good to be happily married, indeed. Its one of the greatest gifts that life can give us, I'm glad we both have it. Let me know when you are able to see me and I'll come and have tea with you. I am very happy about Gwen H. we seem to have 'clicked' at last! To use a vulgar expression.

Well here's my love to you both, especially to you. How's the lad? I've not heard anything about him lately. Yours always,"

In June or early July 1934 he returns to the question of his biography, obviously in response to something Hilda has written to him:

"No I don't want my life written, there's not much to it when one comes to weigh it up. Temper greatly improved, I can't think of much else I have gained in 62 years beyond that.

In proportion to the delightful work which has twice been (placed) on me I seem to have gained very little, perhaps in addition to getting hold of temper I have learned, at least partially, to forgive and not to judge people too harshly. But with such a wonderful and happy occupation I ought to have learned to love people and I haven't except one or two here and there and then only those who loved me.

Sounds like a life largely a failure to me, I wonder if it has been, tho' one learns why I look for death so eagerly. I want to see where I have succeeded and where I've failed if, as I hope, it is possible. And if not and its extinction, I am tired and should not resist extinction at all, tho' I dread the thought of pain and suffering.

I can't think why you should feel miserable at the idea of death, its quite wrong…. By the way, did you ever try to read Whitman? I wish you could, if you have not tried and failed I'll give you the Everyman edition, not as a Birthday present but just as a mental and moral tonic! Let me know if I shall….

One thing I am sure of 'God or no God, future life or no future life' that the strength we need is always there to be reached for and always to be had. I am absolutely certain of this and I mention it so that you may experiment and see if you can't, by reaching for the strength you need, find the strength to finish the day with Tony like something stiffer than a boiled rag… Its quite a good thing to say to oneself 'stiffness' now and again. The form in which I like it best is 'Pray for powers equal to our tasks'.

But I had better stop preaching or you'll leave off writing and what a loss I should feel. I've never had anyone before I really enjoyed writing to or hearing from.

I had a long letter from Gwen…and I wrote her a long letter in reply but Mrs Mathews could not read it and I couldn't rewrite it so I am afraid much of it was lost… "

He was to write to Hilda three more times before he returned home at the end of July. The first letter, on July 9th, was short and chatty:

"I've come to the conclusion that our friendship is a somewhat lopsided one: I always write first!! But as I've been thinking of you all a great deal lately I 'will take up my pen' as our grandfathers (or rather mine) used to say tho' I've nothing much to say unless to remark that 'its damn 'ot and the bathing is lovely', the more so as we've found a much easier place to bathe…

I kept wondering at the beginning of the month how you were enjoying the motor bike and sidecar. Did it come up to your hopes and have you had some good rides? I very much hope so and would like to hear.

I am, thankful to say, rested in mind and body tho' I've got sciatica still… Write and tell me about everything, the boy included. Does he take after his father, and have a gift for the mechanical, or his mother? Have you read anything lately? Do you take any interest in the German situation? It intrigues me greatly...."

And four days later, in response to Hilda who, it is clear, is still finding her two year old a handful:

"You ask me about books about children. Alas, I am very ignorant but if they can't tell you at the Welfare I'll make some enquiries on my return. At least one of my friends will know.

I am sure that the less you say 'don't' and the less you punish the better ((the)) results. A child's naughtiness is really only character development and it must be guided into the right channels and on no account forced. One should, I think, always realise that one is dealing with an undeveloped brain that is feeling its way towards development. I think one may show disapproval without being superior to the child.

I always write about young children with great hesitation I know so little. I think you are wrong about Homer Lane, his principles are, or seem to me, applicable all through. You say he ((the child presumably)) goes about looking for something he ought not to do. As I see it, he goes about looking for some outlet for surplus energy and to find out what happens when he does things.

I am sure no child is consciously naughty, not at this age anyway and I doubt if at all. I would say that the best course is not to take him seriously and to do as we used to say at the office (Leave it to the Lord).

I write these suggestions I all humility as I have not ever had to live with a small child and can know nothing...All I would say is whatever you do don't get annoyed with him. It makes a barrier almost impossible to remove in future years...."

This must have been fairly advanced thinking at the time, but more interesting is the fact that both Frank and Hilda had already given some thought to the teachings of Homer Lane, even if only in the context of an odious but essentially normal two year old. The care and cure of children of with behavioural problems was to occupy Frank for the last decade of his life from his departure from the Invalid Children's Society in 1937 and Hilda for another thirty years after that.

Shortly before the end of his holiday, on July 27th, he replies to a letter from Hilda who has, it seems, touched on the subject of biography again:

"Cae Du, Thursday

You write very nice letters indeed and why on earth you should not write about yourself I can't think. The more you tell me about yourself the more interested I am. So no more of that sort please.

No alas! There are no traces of sainthood or saintliness about me, only the modification of character that old age may, and should, bring. I don't think I am always right, I try to be more patient and more sympathetic. Its easy with those one likes, its so difficult with those one doesn't. But one's a long way off until one has organised the toleration of those who don't do all they should or might, or, rather, those who one thinks don't do so….

Perhaps Tony wants a companion. Have none of your neighbours got babies he can play with? He would quite likely quarrel with this at first but he'd grow out of it. I'm sure ((troublesomeness)) with babies, or anyone else, is want of interest or occupation and a child should learn to find its own interests. Have you thought of trying to teach him his alphabet by way of play and getting him constructive kinds of toys? It would be a good thing to go to a nursery school some time and see the occupations they find there. I'm ashamed to say I've never been, at least for the last 10 years or so. I'll go when I come back if you'll remind me…

I am looking at your letter again and find you ask for criticisms not suggestions. I no longer believe in criticism, only in suggestion. The suggestions themselves should awaken wise self criticism if they are good ones. You should find your own mental tonic and then what little I have done for you will go on with ever increasing force. But if you lean on me, when I go where will you be? And you are not such a soft as to need to lean.

You should lead others and I look to you to do so, so long as you yourself criticise your leading. As to telling you how to 'Look upward', I don't need ((to)). Do it and find yourself the happiness.

I don't know if I have ever told you I wished to start a sect of people who always ask 'Why' when they see one man wants riches, another man is poor, why one man steals, why another lies, another commits murder, another has a happiness we have not achieved, why there is poverty.

'Why' seems to me to be the key to the world's troubles. We would not have any if we always sought the cause of good and of so called evil, we couldn't quarrel, we might, and should, lovingly disagree.

Will you found the sect of 'Whyites' for me? If you don't feel equal to it now do it when I am dead and remember that I look to you to be a leader when your boy is older and you are freer from the world's work.

I am inclined to think you are too parochial in your views. It's a dreadful thing just to live in one's own little circle, and I don't say that you do, but you are so placid that you easily might.

As you keep my letters I am writing this very freely as I wish what I say to last and go on and on in an improved form. Whatever you do, educate your boy if you can so that he grows up with a very broad mind based on love and sympathy….

Alas I've done no climbing, but not because…((I)) don't want to and I've not quite given up all hopes of climbing again if I can get the sciatica cured. It's extraordinary that, tho' I have never been so well, it wont go and I have had to take pills to sleep night after night all the holiday. I can't think why. God knows it's been restful enough and I've had no worry. I've not had any figures sent from the office or any ((papers)) whatever. Still, I'm delightfully well bar those two things.

If I write any more I'll get writer's cramp, and God alone knows what will happen to you trying to read it, so with my best love I am, always yours, FM."

Hilda took his suggestions about child management to heart and attempted to put them into practise, with what end result remains to be seen. But his reading of her character as placid was well off the mark. She may have been able to be relatively easygoing in her personal relationships, though she had a tendency to be stormy with her immediate family, but she found dealing with conflict very stressful. Frank's expressed notion that she could be a leader, in the same way that he undoubtedly was, was wrong: unlike him, she was very good at working toward consensus and could lead from the rear most effectively. She never started another charitable endeavour, let alone a sect, though she did see his last scheme through to completion over very many years. Frank was, it seems plain, projecting his own characteristics on to her either in the hope that she might assimilate them or because he had, consciously at least, missed her real potential. Or, perhaps, he was just trying to keep her on her toes in the expectation that, provided she was not allowed to go to sleep, her potential would eventually be translated into achievement of one sort or another.

No letter from Frank written either at New Year 1935 or during the following summer has survived and, since she kept his letters carefully, it seems likely that he wrote none. It may be that his sciatica stopped him taking his usual month's camping holiday in the summer – his pocket diary suggests a break but, as usual, does not say where.

His next letter, in October 1935 starts with some observations about only having one child – which he seems, on the whole, not to advocate then goes on to assume that she Hilda will have only one:

"…As soon as Tony is old enough I look to see (if I live long enough) you taking some part in public works, helping in Labour Party, learning to speak at meetings … You need, for full development, to live a larger life than that of the home circle. There is no hurry about this but it should be something you are planning for the future when it becomes clearly possible. Why (wait) those two years, (30 instead of 28) you'll soon be 60 and, so far as my experience goes the years from 58 to 64 have been the happiest and most interesting of my life.

I always thought that when I grew old my instincts would dull and my faculties decay. I find myself full of intense and varied interests and, in motoring, I continually improve my driving and my friend T A Leonard who is 5 or 6 years older than I am seems to find life full of interest and useful activities…"

Why he should have chosen the age of 58 as the beginning of his time of greatest happiness and interest can only be guessed at. There was no great change in his family circumstances and he was in the middle of his spell with the Invalid Children's society with Haseley Hall coming along but not yet opened. Hilda left his employment to marry around the time of his 59th birthday and it is possible that he may have been referring, in part, to the development of his friendship with her. Also, he had more money after he was 61, which would have helped. But that doesn't account for the improvement he perceived in his driving which, in later years, matched his temperament in many ways, nor for T A Leonard's experience.

Perhaps Frank has just discovered that life can go on after 60. He concludes by saying that he feels, and for some months has felt himself in perfect health

Frank wrote again at the beginning of December apologising for forgetting Hilda's birthday, as usual, and going on again about the need to do something useful with her life and praising her management of her child. There seems, again, to have been no New Year letter but in July 1936 he is back camping in Wales. Leslie had returned from a walking holiday in Germany with his brother and after commiserating with Hilda, who had shared a holiday cottage in Stow on the Wold in poor weather with her sister in law, he writes:

"… Did he bring any ideas back with him? Has just the lack of language prevented it? … We saw a good deal of two German girls this summer and their outlook gave us the horrors. They completely, or at least one of them did, shut their eyes to all the horrors of modern day Germany and concentrated on the state of Germany in pre Hitler days. Of some of the evils of today's Germany they were curiously ignorant…"

On his birthday in September 1936 he wrote acknowledging good wishes and accepting an invitation to be treated to a performance of 'Things to Come'. (Wells' book had been published in 1933). "provided it did not let you in for too much. If it does let me pay part please." He asked to be told as soon as possible which week it would be so that he and Evelyn could arrange their customary week away in October to fit and to remark that he "can't stand for more than a few minutes without great pain" and that he sees "no hope of getting it cured" since "no one knows the cause". It seems that his sciatica was coming and going, as problems associated with the lower back tend to do in older people.

In February 1937 he wrote from the Carrington Hotel in Criccieth to congratulate Hilda on the news that she was expecting her second child and recommending a couple of books on child psychology and to thank her:

"… for all the things you said about me at the Guild. I love 'a few kind words', as you know and when they are said behind my back I love them more. It has been a very happy association, has it not, and, I believe, will be, as long as I am about. I often wonder how long that will be and find myself dreading the future very much. And yet, I don't see that I could have taken any other course. You will have heard that we have a little over £200 to start with…."

He is referring to his decision to leave the Invalid Children's Society and to the beginning of the final chapter of his working life.

1937 – 1945 NERVOUS CHILDREN

Frank started the Birmingham Society in Aid of Nervous Children in March 1937. The first President was Alderman Harrison Barrow, of a distinguished Quaker family related to the Cadburys, and the first Chairman was Dr C. L. C Burns, the first head of the Birmingham Child Guidance Clinic, now named in his memory. The Clinic had been set up a few years earlier in the department of the City's School Medical Officer to offer psychiatric help to children with nervous or behavioural problems. The relationship that Frank formed with Dr Burns and the clinic was to endure through the history of the Society.

Writing a tribute to Frank in the Society's Report for 1948 – 9, Dr Burns recalled the circumstances:

"Over ten years ago, Frank Mathews started the Birmingham Society in Aid of Nervous Children. He had previously been the originator of a scheme for cripple children which became a vast organisation. He then turned to delicate children who needed convalescent treatment in the country, and built up a scheme based on boarding out in farms. Among these were so-called rheumatic children, for which he also started a residential school. It was the realisation that the great majority of these children with vague pains, 'debility' etc. were quite distinct from the cases of real rheumatic infection which led him on to the next step. It was clear that these were really nervous conditions to a large extent, in other words, emotional problems with physical symptoms. He and I studied the matter and started to send cases from the Child Guidance Clinic to the farms and cottages…."

This collaboration seems to have started before the formation of the new Society. Frank's earlier letters show that he had been interested in child psychology for some years and was familiar with the ideas of Homer Lane by mid 1934. Dr Burns describes the variety of neurotic illnesses in children in the Report of the School Medical Officer for 1936, and though he does not mention farm boarding out it seems clear that he would have been receptive to such an idea and might even already have been experimenting with it

Frank's letter to Hilda in February 1937 implies that he must have decided to start the new Society some time before his resignation from The Invalid Children's Society. By the time his resignation took effect at the end of March he had already gained promises of money and, presumably, other support and Dr Burns had already spoken for six boarding out places. It seems probable that Frank had already started the work of the new Society, perhaps only in a small way, under the aegis of the old.

Over a period of a year or two from 1937 the old Society's farm boarding out was phased out leaving Frank the sole operator of the network of foster homes that he had built up. Before the end of the first year of the new Society Burns was using sixteen places in these homes and was asking for more. Meanwhile, the old Society continued, until it wound itself up in 1941, with Haseley Hall and with placing delicate children in country hospitals and convalescent homes.

A short passage in a letter to Hilda, written in April 1937, suggests that his departure from the old Society had not been all sweetness and light:

> "....your letter left me 'all of a glow'....If only I could believe that this last knock out blow.....may yet bring me the happiness that having the CU ((Cripples Union)) did I would go forward with more courage. But at nearly 66 one does not expect to live long and it seems such a waste to have to stop what one was doing but it could not be considered. I never could do work which appeared to be 'second rate' and I never could work unless there was harmony around me There – I'm talking all about myself, but its no use having children (and surely you are one of mine) if one can't unburden oneself to them. "

Frank had not been in the habit of writing to Hilda about his work problems and that he should do so on this occasion suggests not only that he was seeing her in a new light – as a grown up 'daughter' - but that she may have been party to the events that led up to his move. No doubt, if so, she would have been one of those who encouraged him to start afresh.

Others from the old Society who supported him included Anne Davies, Lilian Davis, Mrs Evans, and Myra Wynn Thomas. All of them joined the founding committee of his new Society which held its first meeting at the Child Guidance Clinic, with Dr Burns in the chair, on 23 June 1937. It was reported at this meeting that 6 children were already away. Florrie West, an old friend from the Cripples Union and committee member of the old Society, joined the Committee.

The choice of the word 'nervous' for the title of the new Society was a carefully considered one. Many of the children who were to be treated could truthfully be described as 'nervous' in the popularly accepted sense – a slamming door might upset them – but others could well have been thought of as badly behaved beyond the normal limits. However, Frank, who had always believed in working with the family rather than with the child alone, would have been anxious to avoid the stigma that would have been associated with any child sent away for bad behaviour, as would Burns, whose approach was necessarily therapeutic. Neither would have wished to lose the sympathy of potential supporters with strong views on law and order. 'Nervous' did very well as a portmanteau description of all.

At first it was thought that the full range of complaints could be usefully addressed using the one method based on country boarding out. Dr Burns set out the rationale in an article in the Birmingham Mail of June 8th 1937 which was reprinted as a preface to the Society's first annual report:

"Whether there are more children nowadays who may be described as being 'nervous' than in previous generations may be left an open question, but there can be no doubt that there is, in our towns, a very large number of children who can be placed in this category.

The description may be a somewhat vague one, but we all know fairly well the type of child that is meant. Here is one definition given by a mother. She said that her child was nervous because 'if he heard a tap running he'd just sob and sob, and if he saw a policeman he'd run a mile!' It is the child who is timorous, who lacks confidence, who feels fear or anxiety, and who shows this attitude outwardly by various habits and disorders such as twitching, night terrors, and other manifestations. He may show it too in his physique – in his tired posture and toneless muscles.

Being hypersensitive to any slight physical disorder he will often complain of vague pains, which may indeed closely resemble rheumatism. But beyond these symptoms there are many forms of behaviour which we now recognise to be, not mere forms of naughtiness, but of emotional disorder, of a neurotic reaction to life (and neurotic after all is but another word for 'nervous'). Temper storms, defiance, truancy, stealing, are often the outward signs of underlying discouragement and unhappiness.

Whatever be the causes, constitutional or environmental, which promote these conditions, it is obvious that the environment of an overcrowded home in the noise and rush of a large town is not the most helpful for their recovery. Also, many of these children come from homes where there is some disharmony or unhappiness which must be held largely responsible for their nervous state. There are today many institutions which help nervous children .... but, working in a Child Guidance Clinic, one finds cases here and there which will not fit into the life of an institution, however perfect a one .... Many of them can be successfully treated by simple methods, or 'grow out of it', but many will continue to lead a semi-invalid, or at least an unhappy, life for months or years and are likely to grow up to swell the large army of neurotic adults, and perhaps of anti-social or criminal types....

These children generally get on better with two or three others in the simple life of a farm or cottage, rather than in any form of institution or in a large group; the object of the Society is therefore to board them out at certain farms which have been selected for the purpose.

The children who are sent will have been carefully chosen on the recommendation of a doctor, and will generally have already received treatment at a hospital or at the Child Guidance Clinic. Thus it will be ensured that every case boarded out will be one that is certain to benefit by this form of treatment; they will be under supervision, and they will not be lost sight of when they return to their homes.

The 'nervous child' has only been recognised and understood within comparatively recent times, but the remedy that we are proposing is an old and tried one; good food, fresh air, the quiet kindly simplicity of life on the land – the way of nature."

The Society sent fifteen children away in its first year, eleven boys and four girls. They were between eight and thirteen years old. One would not settle and returned home almost immediately, one was fetched home by parents after three months, one stayed for over four years.

Five of the fifteen were boarded out with Rosa and Mabel Price, sisters born in 1884 and 1892, who had a smallholding at Aston Munslow on Wenlock Edge in south Shropshire. They had taken children from the old Society from 1928 – at least 50 by 1937 - and were in the habit of looking after a large family, half a dozen or more at a time. Mabel was to die in 1950 but Rosa, who lived into her 90th year, continued with the new Society until boarding out ceased in 1958 by which time she had fostered over 150 children.

Although they looked after more children for The Society than any other foster parents the Price sisters were not generally atypical. They were kind and loving people with a way with children, not very well off and at least partly dependent on the very modest fees paid by the Society. They lived well though with very little luxury. The countryside in which they lived had only the most basic services.

The work of the Society got off to a good start. In the second year a further twelve children were sent to the country and a fifth foster home was added. One girl of 11 was sent to a convalescent home for three months. The children seem to have been a mixed bunch: two subsequently were sent to Approved Schools, two were found to need care directed at their mental handicaps, most of the others progressed to more or less normal lives.

The work was a continuation of the boarding out method that Frank had used for many years for 'invalid' children. Children from the Birmingham area aged between 5 and 16 were put into the care of foster parents in rural areas in the counties of Worcester, Shropshire and Hereford. There they lived a simple family life, attending local schools, for periods ranging from a few months to several years. The foster parents were country people with no special training.

Initially, all these children had first received treatment at the Child Guidance Clinic without satisfactory results and had been referred by Dr Burns who looked on the Society as an extension of the work of the clinic and certainly not a rival method of treatment.

The most difficult problem was to make the treatment effective for children whose troubles were expressed by problematic behaviour. Foster parents had to be taught to understand something about the reasons why the children had been put into their care, but the kindness and reduced tempo of life and removal from some of the environmental causes of unhappiness usually produced improvements while the child was away

Although the basic treatment was simple enough it was only one part of a broad approach to family support which Frank wished to reinforce.

Children referred by the clinic, and, later, by others, were visited and, if foster care was to be offered, the parents were assessed for a contribution toward the cost. This was regarded as an important step, even if the contribution was nominal, as it emphasised that the parents were demanding the treatment and that it was to be a cooperation between the family, the foster parent and the Society rather than being imposed on child and family.

Once a suitable place had been found Frank would take the child to the foster home where he would visit once a month for the duration of the stay. Meanwhile he would visit the family regularly to help with other problems. The parents would be encouraged to visit the foster homes and also to take part in the fund raising and other activities of the Society. After the child's return home regular visits to the family would continue, often for several years, and the child might be allowed to return to the foster home for short or long periods or might even be sent to another foster home.

The aims and methods of the Society were covered sympathetically in the Birmingham Post and the Birmingham Mail – even the idea of treating rather than punishing delinquents seemed to raise no hackles – and many prominent citizens lent their support or donated money.

Income in the first year was £794, more than a tenth coming from parents' contributions, and the first list of subscribers and donors included many of Frank's longstanding friends and supporters. Family support came from Ethel Mathews and Winifred Holden as well as from A Holden and Sons, and contributing friends included T A Leonard, Sir Walford Davies (Anne's brother) and Myra Wynn Thomas. The Ivy Fellowship gave £51, the Womens' Guild £33 and the Birmingham Mail Christmas Tree Fund £21. Miss Robins, the Society's Treasurer, gave £12 and Mr and Mrs Barrow Cadbury £10. Mrs Cadbury, who had been an early supporter of the Child Guidance Clinic, also sent a letter of support based on her experience as a City Magistrate.

Early in 1938 Gwen Hazelwood was appointed as Frank's secretary at £2 –10 – 0 per week and the Society took a room for an office at 23 Laburnum Road, just round the corner from the Mathews' house, at ten shillings per week to include cleaning. The house was rented from the Bournville Village Trust by Mr and Mrs Wheelwright whose daughter Dorothy had been a patient of and worked at The Woodlands.

Income in the second year rose to £1031, including £20 from a radio appeal by Dr Burns, and it was recorded that some money had been set aside toward a small home. Though symptoms of delinquency frequently cleared up while children were with the foster parents they sometimes came back when they returned to their families. It already seemed likely that some of the more disturbed children would need more therapy than foster parents could provide.

Frank, meanwhile, seemed to be much happier than he had been. On June 24th 1938 he wrote to Hilda from The Skelwith Bridge Hotel, Ambleside:

> "Its about time I wrote to and had a letter from you. I seem to see so little of you since the novelette arrived, nice as she is to look at. I wish it were possible to find a 'self raising' powder for babies like there is for bread. This putting to bed between six and seven puts me out: I can't drop in for a chat, or I can drop in but can't get the chat.
>
> I've not much news. I had a very delightful seven days at Capel Curig and to my delight found myself walking better and more easily than I have for ten years. I did Snowdon in three and a half hours instead of five and Glydyr in two and a half instead of four…
>
> It was a good move getting Gwen as my secretary, life is almost enjoyable again and I am surprised to find how well she can plan and do things without any suggestion or supervision from me. I knew she was conscientious but I did not realise how capable…"

The 'novelette' was Hilda's daughter who had arrived the previous August and whose first name had been inspired by a character in fiction too light to meet with Frank's approval. Her second name was Evelyn. The times for the climbs were at least respectable for a man of nearly 70. It is hard to believe that the disappearance of Frank's sciatica, which did not return, had nothing to do with his change of direction. He could never have achieved what he did if he had allowed doubts to sap his energy and it may be that his tiredness and niggling physical problems over the preceding ten years had something to do with an inner feeling that he was not doing the best that he could.

The Society's second year was the last to be completed before the start of the second world war. Frank was much too old to be directly involved in any fighting as were most of the people working for the Society. Hilda, with two young children, was unlikely to be called up, other younger workers had medical conditions that precluded heavy work. Even Leslie at 33 would not be among the first to be called into the armed forces. There seemed no reason why the Society would not be able to continue with its work even if war came. War would have seemed unlikely to make the need for it less pressing.

Nevertheless, Frank, like many people, was intensely worried by the prospect of war. In a long letter to Hilda, mainly about books he had been reading, he digressed to set out his position:

"Glasfryn, Llwyngwril, 2 October 1938

…I also was very interested in A. R. P. ((air raid precautions)) by Haldane tho' part of it was so terrible I had to skip it…

As to pacifism, I can't agree with you. I think the sacrifices it involves are enormous and very very hard to make but they are in no way accompanied with any evil, while war never accomplishes that which it sets out to do under any circumstances and…is always accompanied by every possible kind of evil, in thought and action, and hatches another war after it is completed. War is the abnegation of Reason.

Surely one must use Reason in every compartment of life. At one time men used to fight each other when they could not decide what was right. Now they go to law. The same applies to towns. They used to fight each other but found it useless. Do you think for a moment that, if statesmen who find it difficult to decide a question…would have to fight and be killed, they would turn to war?

I agree that we pacifists would let the world get into what looked like a pretty mess if we were able to carry out our ideas, but it would be a mess out of which the phoenix of reason, love and law would ultimately come.

If it is true that evil can never beget anything but evil it is equally true that the Right course invariably brings Good. It may not be apparent for a long time but it is in the very long run.

Once you have decided that 'war accomplishes nothing' one just has to keep repeating that fact to oneself until it becomes part of oneself as it ultimately must. Why even consider a thing which accomplishes nothing and is accompanied by every evil under the sun?…

I think that expresses my thoughts on the matter. I may have repeated myself but that wont matter will it?…"

Fortunately for many people Frank had never been in the habit of allowing practical considerations to cloud what he felt was right, nor did he always consider counter arguments as carefully as he might have done. Nevertheless, the prospect of war troubled him a great deal and he continued to discuss his own reaction to it with Hilda.

In his birthday letter to her in November 1938 he wrote of his pleasure in her having worked her way round to pacifism – Evelyn never did – and a few days later he emphasised his own position again:

"This is not really a proper letter, only just an answer to a query of yours.

I would not buy the 5/- Grey book till you have sampled the pamphlets of his. I have one if not two in a batch of pamphlets the P.P.U. ((Peace Pledge Union)) sent me and I did not take to Grey at all. He's a Quaker and I dislike Quakers and their writings tho' I'm very likely quite wrong…. Do please get the pamphlets and give me a good lambasting if I'm allowing my prejudices to affect my judgement. Only I'm a little afraid you may become a Quaker and if you do all the piquancy and sauce will go out of my life….even if you become a Quaker after I'm dead I'll come back and haunt you and in a very sentimental way…"

It is interesting that Frank should express so strong an antipathy to Quakers – or perhaps Quakerism. He had been supported in his work by the Cadbury family and other Birmingham Quakers almost from the very first and he had chosen to live in Bournville, founded by George Cadbury and with a strong Quaker ethic. Clearly he shared many Quaker attitudes to social questions. There must have been something about their religious position that he did not care for or possibly he is thinking specifically of the Quaker response to war, which permits such things as the Friends Ambulance Unit. Still, he admits that his attitude may be related to his prejudices and that he may be quite wrong.

When he wrote to Hilda for her birthday in November 1939 the war had been going on for three months, albeit without much action in the West. Pacifism was still to the front of his mind. In a long letter mainly about books read he says:

> "Its good that you and I are one about pacifism, and that there are many young people in your set who are, makes me feel the world is getting better in spite of appearing to get worse.
>
> What about the idea of Federation that is so much in the air just now? It seems to me that what killed the League of Nations will prevent the 'Federation of Nations', Capitalism and Fachism (sic). Where are Italy, Germany and Spain going to fit in, let alone Russia. Will Russia federate with capitalism?
>
> By the way, what's the difference between a constructive pacifist and a religious one and which am I? I can see the difference, possibly we want a definition of what is religion…"

* * *

The war, when it came, did not at first greatly affect the Society's work. In the third year's report (1939-40) Frank was able to report that the number of children away had risen from 16 to 24 and that many people had written saying that the work was specially needed in time of war. The authorities had agreed to pay maintenance for children sent away from evacuable areas thus saving the Society £80 in the first half year.

Income for the year was £1,228, mostly from the usual sources and including £203 in parents' payments. But the income and expenditure account shows one novel item, £130 profit on sales of diary calendars.

In November 1939 Frank reported to his committee that 25,000 diary calendars had been printed, for about £30 judging by the printing and stationery bill for the year, and that he hoped to raise £100 by selling them to the public. These calendars, were optimistically described as 'diary calendars'.

They were about three inches by two with a double page for each month and four pages of text about the Society's work. The front cover had a decorative design – for some reason a design featuring a black cat always sold best – and the back showed the price – twopence at first – and gave the Society's name and address.

This rather unlikely seeming venture prospered from the start and was to be repeated for almost twenty years. Early each autumn samples were received from the printer and sent out to distributors – often charity representatives in factories or other workplaces – who returned their orders. The main order was, in due course, delivered to the Mathews' house in boxes of a thousand calendars where it took up most of the hallway and front room. Each day a group of volunteers would meet to count out the orders and make them into neat parcels for the post, wrapped in brown paper, tied with string and sealed with wax. Within ten years well over 100,000 calendars were being sold each year and the year's profit exceeded £1,000. This was to have a profound effect on Frank's ability to move on to his next venture.

Meanwhile, in its third year, the Society had a surplus of £127. While remarking on this the report was at pains to damp down any overconfidence. It was suggested that things might not continue so well because "in war time incomes are trebly uncertain" – a worry that was not to be substantiated by events – and also that "our Honorary Secretary, who started and directs the Society, is no longer young, and it is therefore doubtful for how long he will be able to carry on.

Should he have to retire it is very important that there should be a substantial sum in hand until the conditions of the work could be readjusted."

The Annual Report for the fourth year (1940-41) was only eight pages long, the committee having decided to save paper by omitting lists of donors and subscribers for the duration of the war. Nevertheless, space was found for a look at what had been achieved:

"In our earlier reports we have suggested that the work which we started out to do was experimental. Although we have only just completed our fourth year, we can look back and say that the result of our experiment has been highly satisfactory. We cannot look back to 100 percent of successes, but we can say that in a very difficult task the successes are far in excess of the failures, and that these failures are merely stepping stones to ultimate success.

We begin to realise our problem and to know that when the war is over we can hope to reduce our failures by the addition of a small Home of our own where the more difficult cases can be treated....

In the Report of the School Medical Officer to the City Education Committee, Dr Burns says: 'The beneficial effects of the Boarding out of selected cases in properly chosen and supervised Foster Homes needs no stressing. We have also been fortunate in carrying on our collaboration with the Society in Aid of Nervous Children. There are at present 26 children boarded in six different farms. The type of case for each Foster Home is selected partly according to the personality of the people who will be in charge of them. Mr Mathews, the Hon. Secretary has been indefatigable in continuing his visits to the farms, keeping careful notes of each case and discussing progress constantly with the ((Child Guidance)) Clinic Director. The results are outstandingly successful, and one feels no hesitation in saying that in several very difficult cases even the most highly specialised treatment in a Home could not have produced a quicker or more striking result'..."

Obviously Dr Burns would have wished to stress the positive outcome of many of the cases treated but it is clear from Frank's reference to the need for a home for the more difficult cases that Frank and he had already realised that the improvements produced while a child was away were not always maintained after return and that in some cases a more intensive method of treatment would be needed.

The finances continued to be healthy, though the report again cautioned against complacency. Income for the year was £1348, including £160 from calendars, and there was a surplus of £203. Gwen Hazelwood was appointed Assistant Secretary.

A footnote to this report gives news of Frank's former society:

> "Since this report was written the Society for the care of Invalid Children has decided to amalgamate with this Society, handing over to the Education Committee the work which it was doing at Haseley Hall. The Boarding Out work which had to be given up through lack of funds will be revived by the amalgamated Society. We are glad to say that several member of the Committee of the Invalid Children's Society are joining that of this Society, which will be known in future as the Birmingham Society for the Care of Invalid and Nervous Children.."

In a letter to Hilda written at New Year 1941 Frank put it differently:

> "...Did Gwen tell you the 'Invalid Children' are closing down, giving Haseley to the Education Committee? Miss Moore ((the Superintendent)) left directly she heard of this. They have only a deficit of about £170 on the year's working and lots of money on deposit and quite £2,000 invested. A scandal is it not? Roberts ((the Chairman)) has got tired of it and is afraid of being responsible for the rent of Haseley as he is a trustee. I am going to try and stage a sham amalgamation so as to pick up the income they have left. It must be nearly £3,000, well over £2,000. It's a good thing after all that Gwen came to me. (Virtue does get rewarded sometimes.) The others will all be sure to get jobs but they won't be as interesting..."

Somehow, the tone is not as regretful as might have been expected. The combined Society's income for the following year did not reflect anything like the £2,000 he had hoped for nor does he seem to have come in for any of the invested money. Spare furniture from the amalgamation was used to furnish a small upstairs room at Laburnum Road for Frank's use. The rent for this was 3/6 per week.

Late in 1940 Hilda had taken the two children and had gone with her mother to live in rented rooms in a farmhouse in north Herefordshire, Leslie remaining in Birmingham to work. Although bombing in the suburbs had not been heavy the sleepless nights and constant threat had taken their toll and there was no sign of a let up. Frank was delighted at the thought of them living in a beautiful area that he knew well and he rightly believed that the children would benefit from the experience – even if he had a rather sentimental view of life in the deep countryside. His own mood, however was not cheerful:

"Early 1941, Bournville

….I'm glad Les is happy, well and facing the future in the same brave way you do…I'm very well tho' I don't find anything in life to make me want to go on living, I wish I needn't…Anyway, I found the old horoscope the other day – the one I had done at eighteen – and it said I'd live to 76 and its always been correct to two years so here I remain I'm afraid…"

He was 69. And a month or so later:

"Bournville, 8 April 1941

You will think I don't appreciate your very nice letter taking, as I have, a month to answer it. But, truth to tell, I've been so depressed this last month that I've lost all hope and find life unbearable. I've given up listening to the news and only glance at the headlines in the Manchester Guardian and read only reviews in the New Statesman. I don't remember feeling as badly in the last war, tho' one felt very bad then, so I've found it difficult to write and my work is not done as well as it should be. Its fortunate that I have Gwen, she is a help and comfort and…never grumbles.

I need a few days climbing, I don't know what I wouldn't give for a few days alone in the mountains.

No we did not go away at Easter, they couldn't take us at Solva and I won the excuse not to spend the money.

Things were not too good with us financially but miraculously they've cleared up for the time being at any rate. I wonder did I tell you how old Mrs Julia left me £100 all for myself, not for the Society? I expect I did but it's so long since we met that time seems non existent. Is it possible to get a good supper and breakfast anywhere in your neighbourhood? If we could we would fit it in with a round and spend an evening with you.

I've been looking for Leinthall on the map. There seem to be two, L. Starkes and L. Earls. Are you at either or in between or where? What a lovely life for the children and how clearly you make me see it in your letter. It's lovely to think that many children are benefiting from the war, if many are suffering. One wonders what effect it will have on children's lives when the war is over.

I wonder very much, for the stay at Haseley, altho' so unique in its best days, had little or no lasting effect. No child kept up its interest in music or love of the country so far as I could see, yet in the early days the little cottage home we had at Chadwick End had a very lasting effect on a fair number of the children. But that was 40 years ago.

No, I have no hope of a ((quick)) ending of the war, how I wish I had….In respect of the war, I do believe that this cataclysm will lead to a different world but I don't think it will do so quickly. You may live to see the beginning of it. I know I won't and I dread the interim so. But I was always a coward in one way, I have always been able to do the difficult thing but have never yet been able to do it cheerfully or hopefully.

I'll show you my horoscope some time. It has the descriptions of seven women who would influence my life and the descriptions are recognisable. It tells me which of them I would not marry. There were two I might. I …. missed one and did marry the other,

I'm glad to say for whatever upsets I may have had in my life my marriage is not one of them…."

The letter ends, more cheerfully than it starts, with a reference to the Society's £130 surplus for the year which he describes as 'miraculous'.

By the middle of August Frank had refreshed himself and seemed in a buoyant mood:

"Bournville, 16 August 1941…..

I had one of the most delightful holidays of my life this year. Evelyn and I went to Llanfairfechan ((by road))…The Leonards were going for a week and wanted us to meet them there – but it ((the Cooperative Holidays Association guest house)) turned out to be a peacefully glorious situation two miles up hill out of Llanfairfechan with a kind of terraced garden looking out onto green mountains on one side and the Menai Straits on the other. The walks were very limited but so enjoyable they could be done twice and each week someone took us in tow and made us join them in walks…

Mrs Mathews even got to the top of Drum, about 2,500 ft but you could almost take a perambulator up it!! There is a very lovely view, from the top, of the country I love so much, the Glyders and Carnedds.

We had glorious weather, little or no rain and lovely golden evening effects on the mountains and strait and there was plenty to eat considering the times.

We came home for a week and then I went to Capel ((Curig)) and had one of the most wonderful weeks I've ever had anywhere. Climbed 5 mountains in 6 days and did a good afternoon walk on the odd day. What's more I climbed more easily than I have for 20 years and on the first three climbs knocked an hour off my previous times and never knew what it was to be tired or stiff even tho' on the last day I had a one and a half hour walk up the Llanberis Pass road.

I've not lost the good of it yet, physically or mentally…..((it's)) so lovely to be alone in country I have a real passion for. It's a disgraceful thing to say but I found, or thought I found, more pleasure in a week's climbing than in a year's work, even though the work is so useful. I am ashamed, but there it is. I can't think why mountains mean so much to me…"

By this time Hilda had moved, with the children and her mother, to a tiny cottage in farm land four miles from Bromyard in Worcestershire. The cottage had no immediate neighbours, was a mile across fields from the nearest village and four miles from the nearest shops where all supplies except milk and bread had to be bought. Curiously, there was a recent bomb crater in the field behind.

It was an idyllic setting for a long hot summer, though hard work, but, with no outside contact except a radio whose lead acid battery had to be carried weekly into town to be recharged, it did not present a prospect that Hilda felt she could endure through a hard winter. Obviously she had told Frank of her doubts:

"Bournville 2nd September 1941

I was so glad to have your letter even if it was such an unhappy one. There is little I can say to comfort you in these dark days but I thought I would copy out two poems that I resort to myself when things look very black. I'm not sure if you'll like them but expect you will…The first I don't know where I picked it up. I thought it was in the old Labour Church Hymn Book…:

' When head and hand and heart are weary
When hope with folded wings sinks out of sight
Etc'

The other is by Lewis Morris:

'It is not best in an inglorious cause to sink in dull content
…'

(later that day) There has been a long interval since I wrote that as I got out my newspaper cutting book (started in 1890) to verify Lewis Morris' poem. But I found early Cinderella Appeals and Reports and so wallowed in the past instead of writing to you.

I've just had your nice birthday note and like to have it very much – you know how I like to be made a fuss of by those I love. If there is a cheap edition of Mr Polly by Wells I'd love to have it, I'd like it the more if it had your name in it.

I don't know I want to live much longer. I don't know that I want to go on living at all but that glorious holiday I had, especially the week's climbing, seems to have helped me very greatly in that respect. I've not thought how much I wanted to die often for 4 or 5 days together and when I do the longing is not so intense. I'm really ashamed of myself... So take an example by me and go to Leighton Buzzard however difficult it is to arrange...it would be good to go without the children..."

The bombing had become much less frequent and intense and Hilda was anxious to return to Birmingham before winter arrived. But she had nowhere to go: the house she and Leslie owned in Hall Green had been let to a colleague of his.

Fortunately, Leslie was able quite quickly to find a house to rent and she and the children returned to join him in the suburb of Kings Heath, quite close to Frank's centre of operations in Bournville

After that letters were fewer and further between partly because Frank and Hilda soon started to see each other more often. Once Valerie was five years old and had started school Hilda was able to help in the Society's office for a few hours per week and in the Report for 1942 – 43 it was announced that she had been appointed Honorary Financial Secretary of the Society. In the same Report it was announced that Janet McCrindell, a member of the Committee, had been appointed Secretary with a view to her becoming Frank's successor.

This was not Frank's first attempt to put a successor in place. In October 1942 an attempt was made to appoint a Miss Mayhew as

Secretary at a salary of £300. Negotiations were successful and she was to have started on 1st April but at a Committee meeting on 16th March 1943 it was revealed that Miss Mayhew had been forced to decline because she had been unable, under wartime regulations, to obtain release from the teaching profession. Miss McCrindell offered, at this meeting, to take on the job for six months at the same salary and her offer was accepted on the spot.

Meanwhile Frank had started to prepare for the home he hoped to open after the war. He announced in February 1943 that he was to visit Dunmow Hall in Clitheroe, Yorkshire and Barnes House Manor in Peebles. At the latter he would have met W David Wills who was becoming well known for his progressive methods of helping children with behavioural problems, much along the lines pioneered by Homer Lane. Within a few months Dr Burns and Miss McCrindell had both visited Dunmow and Barnes and Frank had talked about his scheme with Birmingham's Chief School Attendance Officer and the Chief Probation Officer. The Home Fund was augmented thanks to a profit of £1,100 on the sale of calendars.

There was a setback at the end of the financial year when Miss McCrindell resigned as Secretary the reason given being that "arrangements had not developed as anticipated", though she would remain a member of the Committee. Frank seems to have been relieved. Writing to Hilda from Conway on January 24th 1944 he said:

> "…I too am very happy and for the first time since last April am not dreading returning home. In fact, if Evelyn will get well in time I'm looking forward to it.
>
> I'm full of plans and so thankful the McCrindell regime is coming to a close and I hope a friendly one too. I had a very interesting time with the doctors at Hagley Road on Wednesday. Both were very friendly and interested and suggested it might be possible to take over one of their homes after the war. They've promised to let me see 3 of them very soon too.

I'm going to London to see what I can do about someone trained, or partially trained, to take part of Miss McCrindell's work (or rather the work she should have done if she had been capable of taking over). Then in the next few months, anyway soon after Miss McCrindell has gone, you are to be Hon. Secretary along with me and to be in charge of the Society, and of the paid Secretary, when I give up.

I hope you will agree to this, which has been in my mind for a long time, and to my great delight Mrs Mathews suggested the same thing to me…"

Given his high opinion of Hilda it is hardly astonishing that Frank should consider her as a possible successor. She was the right age, 37, and her children were in school and would become more self reliant. Frank had never made any secret of his hope that she would, at the right time, broaden her horizons. It is hard to say whether she would have been better able to cope with his job than Miss McCrindell, given that she was not Frank.

He seems to have got quite a long way in his planning without telling her and her reply seems to have conveyed the message that he should hold his horses. He must have realised that he had some persuading to do and on January 30th, the day before his return to Birmingham he wrote again:

"I was very glad to get your letter.

No ((I)) will not rush the Hon Secretaryship at all and there is no need to as long as I keep well and work and feel like working a little longer. But it is a great relief to feel that I can actually make you my successor, instead of hoping you will be, and appointing a social worker to be 'under' solves all the problems if we get the right social worker…"

The appointment of a social worker took longer than expected, the job not being filled until March the next year. Meanwhile, Frank continued to make progress with the 'home'.

In June he reported to the Committee on four more visits by him to hostels and special schools and on a visit by Hilda and Evelyn to Barnes. He consulted the Ministry of health for advice and, on 14th November outlined his plans for the 'home' to the Committee.

It was obvious that David Wills' work at Barnes interested him greatly so it is, perhaps, not surprising that he took the bold step in January 1945 of making an 'advance appointment' of Wills at a salary of £400 per annum – to include the services of Mrs Wills – to take effect when Wills was ready, possibly at the end of the year.

In the Annual Report of the Society for 1944 – 45, its eighth year of existence, Frank reported that, partly thanks to another £950 from the calendars, over £5,000 was now in hand for the proposed "country school" and that David Wills had "consented to act as Warden". A social worker had been appointed to do home visiting and Frank felt able to make the remarkable statement that in the whole of the Society's history he had "never known what it is to be short of money".

Although there is no evidence that Frank ever changed his view about war in general and the second world war in particular he had seen, quite early on, that the upheaval would have far reaching, and in many cases beneficial, social effects. The way in which he was able to bring in sufficient money for his purposes reflected the new level of employment and the shortage of things to spend wages on but it also owed something to changed attitudes to social problems which would greatly help Frank's endeavours.

Other, larger scale, influences were also soon to come into play. These included the passing of the 1944 Education Act which, when it came into force, would govern the enterprise he was planning, and the election of a government whose philosophy rested heavily on the social principles he had long held. Frank was closer to the mainstream than he had ever been.

1945 – 1948 HANDING OVER

Having, in effect, taken out an option on David Wills, Frank and his Committee set about the practicalities of getting a Country School started. First of all, this meant finding somewhere to start it.

It was proposed that the school would be for about thirty maladjusted boys and girls who would need living accommodation and schoolrooms. As the school would be in the countryside most, if not all, the staff would live in, at least until things settled down.

Local Authorities had been given the duty under the 1944 Education Act to provide suitable education for maladjusted children. The provision could include boarding education in private establishments run by charities such as the Birmingham Society for the Care of Invalid and Nervous Children. The authorities would pay the day to day costs, by paying fees, provided that the school, which must be registered and would be subject to inspection, met the standards set down by government. Central government had the power to provide a grant in aid as a contribution to the capital costs.

Local and central government funding would be crucial, for the Society, for all its success, could not hope to find more than a fraction of either the capital or the running cost of a Country School. Frank was no stranger to public funding – the teaching costs at the Woodlands, the Forelands and Haseley Hall had all been contributed to by the educational authorities at the time – but previously it had always been a case of public money being a useful, perhaps even a necessary, addition to the Society's funds. This time it was to be the other way round; especially because of the high ratio of staff to children needed for its difficult task. The cost per child would be much greater than that of Frank's earlier ventures. Also, the regulations under which it would be run were much more stringent than hitherto: to comply with them would add to the complexity and cost of the organisation required. The school would exist only if the authorities wanted it and would, and could, pay for it.

The term 'maladjustment' had only been widely adopted in Britain after the second world war and it was generally admitted at the time to be unsatisfactory. In 1950 the Ministry of Education was to set up a Committee to report on the problem of maladjustment in children. Its report, issued in 1955, goes into the question 'what is maladjustment?' at some length. In an appendix it summarises a grouping of symptoms which "may be indicative of maladjustment". The list, which was generally used by child guidance clinics, includes nervous disorders, habit disorders, behaviour disorders, organic disorders, psychotic behaviour, educational and vocational difficulties and "unclassified". Pilot studies based on evaluations of children by parents and teacher suggested, or seemed to suggest, that something like one in ten of the school population was probably maladjusted and that three or four in every thousand children needed special treatment. Clearly, anyone trying to help maladjusted children was faced with both a slippery concept and a big problem.

By the time the government Committee was set up Frank had been helping maladjusted children for a dozen years though, rather than use a term that neither he nor anyone else could define, he would speak in terms of the symptoms of individuals or groups. He had understood early on, however, that his boarding out method, did not always produce sustained improvements and he had seen the need for some of his children to receive regular psychiatric help as well as a change of environment and the support he could offer to them and their families. At the Country School these children, who would have been among the three or four per thousand identified in the Committee's report, would receive that expert help.

Compared with what was to follow, finding a place for the school turned out to comparatively straightforward. After one false start, when a property was rejected because of a bad surveyor's report, the Society's Committee agreed in February 1946 to take an option on

Bodenham Manor, a large country house in the Jacobean style. The purchase was completed on the 7th November for a price of £5,000, most of the money that had been set aside.

The land on which the house stood was once part of a large estate indentured to Sir Thomas Coningsby in 1597 but the first mention of Bodenham Manor in the deeds was not until 1923. The deeds do not say when the house was built but its style suggests the late nineteenth or early twentieth century. Immediately before the Society bought it the house was occupied by a religious community.

It had nineteen acres of grounds, mostly rough hillside woodland and was thought to be ideal for the purpose. It would provide most of the living accommodation and a stable block could be converted to schoolrooms and additional dormitories. There was a large kitchen garden that would provide all the fresh vegetables. The nearest large town was Hereford, about six miles away, but the house was reasonably accessible from Birmingham, about an hour and a half away by car.

Frank was keen to get the school going, worried that the available money would be eaten up by commitments, and impatient of delay. In April 1945 he wrote to Hilda:

"6 Lancaster Square, Conway

…I had a letter from David asking for a substantial allowance as well as the £400 p.a. (He is getting £400 p.a. is he not?) I am somewhat bothered by this as we, or rather I, foolishly appointed a gardener as well from early in April and all this will have to come out of capital. Can you let me have a statement of the exact position, or as near exact as possible, of the money available for Bodenham after the house has been bought. How much is left, or, rather, what is left in the calendar fund available for Bodenham etc.

Gwen sent me a letter this morning saying the March income was 'not too good' instead of giving me the approximate figures. Are they very bad? Its disappointing, as she should know by now of my liking for the actual figures, not careless statements like that.

We have had a very nice time here and I am much better but not nearly so much as I hoped. Two miles is my limit or I get so tired and wake tired and somewhat dread the next few months' work. I have told David I propose going to London to see Bosworth Smith and get to know the exact position, what we can expect from the Ministry ((Education)) and whether we cannot start at once with just a few children. I'm sick of all this guess work and his friend, who knows Bosworth Smith, says the present is not a time for him to intervene…"

The proposed meeting with the Ministry seems to have taken place with David Wills in attendance but with mixed results. The internal papers of the Ministry are now open and it is possible to see from them that the civil servants were keen to approve Bodenham Manor as a special school but were doubtful, to say the least, about the main protagonists.

A minute dated June 1946 summarises the view held at that time about approval and the necessary finance:

> The Birmingham Society for the Care of Invalid and Nervous Children have acquired a property known as Bodenham Manor, near Hereford, for the purpose of establishing a school for 30 maladjusted children. The Society have paid £5,000 for the freehold of the house and nearly 20 acres. The District Valuer … gives the 1939 value as £4,500 and the current value as £5,000.

> There is, as I think you know, very little residential special school provision in the country for maladjusted children, and for some little time to come we cannot expect Local Education Authorities to do much in the way of providing such schools, though Authorities are only too anxious to send children to them where they exist and every such school has a long waiting list. We should therefore like to encourage voluntary bodies to go ahead, and though we have some misgivings about details in this particular case, I have no doubt that we ought to approve the

school as a special school and to take care, once it is started, to see that it is run on the best possible lines. This will be done by frequent inspections in the early stages, and we shall keep a pretty close hold on the Managers.

We cannot actually make an accommodation grant until the Trust Deed has been drawn up, constituting the Trustees and dealing with the managing body, but I should be grateful if you would obtain Treasury consent to our making an accommodation grant when these formalities are completed.

I should be grateful, too, for your advice on the following point. The Managers have capital assets of about £7,200, and their total commitments for purchase, equipment and enlargement of the school comes to something over £14,500. They are therefore asking for an accommodation grant of £7,500 towards these three objects. I suggested that they should raise part of the balance by mortgage on the premises and charge the loan charges in the fees payable by Local Education Authorities. You will see from the letters immediately preceding this that the Managers have a horror of "getting into debt" or "saddling themselves with a large debt". Possibly they have not realised that the whole of the loan charges could be covered by the approved fees, though this was fully explained to Mr. Mathews, the Secretary. However this may be, the Managers are very anxious to have no capital liabilities, while they are fully prepared to subsidise the maintenance costs out of voluntary funds. I imagine that they will go on collecting subscriptions year by year and by this means will keep the fee appreciably below the actual cost. On the whole, though I should have preferred a loan, I don't think we can stand out for this and accordingly, subject to your views, and of course to getting clear facts about the financial position, I am inclined to offer a grant of £7,000, or not exceeding £7,500 if their total expenditure justifies this amount.

Another minute, of January 1948, dealing mainly with details of the grant that was to be offered reveals the civil servants' feelings about the people (some manuscript abbreviations have been filled out):

You will remember this troublesome case. The history is briefly that the Birmingham Society for the Care of Invalid & Nervous Children wanted to set up a school for maladjusted. Children. They bought a house in Herefordshire called Bodenham Manor … we agreed, after Mr. Pearson had referred to the Treasury, to give an accommodation grant of £7,500 …

Unfortunately the cost on tender of the adaptations has proved much more than was anticipated. The estimate for the work is now £23,600. I don't think we can keep the Managers waiting another year if we are going to approve at all. They are being put to considerable expense in maintaining Bodenham Manor & they engaged the Warden ... long ago, though the latter is their affair.

The Warden, as you know, is one of the snags in this case as we do not feel happy about his suitability. Nor do we like Mr. Mathews the Hon. Sec. of the Society. He is however 75 & in all fairness to the remaining members of this society I do not think that we should judge them on Mr. Mathews. Mr. Austin the Chairman of this Society (who came here for an interview on 27.11.47 with Mrs. Reed) struck me as a very sensible level headed kind of man. The President of this Society, Alderman Harrison Barrow is a well known Birmingham figure, much in civic business & Dr. Burns, their psychiatrist, & the Birmingham Child Guidance M.O. is, Sir Alfred & Mr. Lumsden tell me, quite sound.

I mention this because I think we have been rather swayed by Mr. Mathews & Mr. Wills. The latter is undoubtedly a problem but you will remember that Mr. Bosworth Smith made enquiries about him & afterwards agreed to let the (scheme)... go ahead

Were it not for Mr. Mathews & Mr. Wills I feel that this scheme is as worthy of consideration as Arlington Manor, Newbury. Schools for maladjusted are almost as desperately needed as schools for the deaf as is borne out by our recourse to ... assistance to independent schools – most necessary for maladjusted cases....

Do you think it would be any harm to ask the Chairman of the Society (Mr. Austin who came up on the 27/11 about the plans) & Mrs. Rees who is the paid secretary to come and see us? Perhaps it would be difficult to ask the paid official & better to try to get the President (Alderman Harrison Barrow). I suggest this because if you agree that we can't go back on what we've done already towards setting this school up, it would be better to have a frank discussion at the beginning... The great stumbling block is Mr. Wills....I think we should avoid having Mr Mathews at any interview. I feel that any others could (not be) frank in front of him. He is 75 now and it is to be hoped will drop out of things before long but of course these impossible old folk often go on for years!..."

The distrust of David Wills seems to have originated at the first meeting with Wills and Frank in early 1945 and to have been reinforced by a discussion with the officials' Scottish counterparts. This discussion took place in November 1945. An official of the Scottish Education Department (Wills work at Barnes came under Scottish jurisdiction) is reported to have said that:

"In addition to receiving information from various sources ((he)) visited the hostel once and thus gained first-hand impressions of Mr. Wills. The latter believed in very free discipline which in some respects did not conform to ordinary school standards, e.g. the children need not wash their hands before meals if they did not wish to do so, no form of punishment was meted out for misdeeds and an undue familiarity between him and them was permitted. He was somewhat self-opinionated in that he did not consider that he had anything to learn from persons engaged in similar work.

((He)) sensed a feeling of suspicion and mistrust about Mr. Wills and his methods and thought he was being untrue to himself. He did not think Mr. Wills was actually dishonest judging from his own peculiar standards but there was something indefinitely wrong which suggested that Mr. Wills was not suitable for dealing with children. Opinions varied about him from that suggesting that he did produce some ... results with a few of the children to that asserting that he was a hypocrite. ((He)) favoured one midway between these two, but he definitely considered that employment of Mr. Wills should be approved only with the greatest caution."

It is, perhaps, not astonishing that civil servants of the 1940's should be shocked by David Wills' methods. Their own education would probably have been entirely traditional and there would have been no requirement for the people administering the government's policy for the treatment of maladjusted children to know anything much about the subject. That they should have been prepared to judge his personal suitability on the basis of their own and their colleague's impressions is, perhaps, shocking to a present day observer.

To be fair, they did not let their feelings get in the way of supporting the idea of Bodenham Manor as a special school though they did worry a lot among themselves about whether they should approve the appointment of Wills as Warden and this may well have been at least part of the reason that it was five years after the purchase of the house before the School actually opened.

In February 1948 it seems to have been decided that the delays had been sufficient and authorisation was sought within the Ministry, and obtained, for work on the buildings to start in the second half of the year. A first payment of £3,000, toward the cost of buying the property, was acknowledged by Hilda in October and shortly afterwards it was recognised within the Ministry that, since Wills was to be Warden and not a teacher, there was no power to approve or disapprove his appointment. The scheme went ahead subject to later review and to stipulations as to the age ranges of children to be taken.

A few hours of homework would have saved the officials from embarrassingly misjudging Frank – though he would not have cared. Fortunately, they seem to have suffered from a collective delusion that Frank didn't matter and that the Committee could be relied on to see things through. He gave a discrete account of what had gone on in the Society's Annual Report for 1947 – 48:

"...At the beginning of the Report I said how sorry I was not to have published a Report for two years. But these last two years have been a series of one dashed hope after another. We have kept on hoping that in six months or so we would be able to open Bodenham Manor as a Residential School for the more difficult children. At one time we were so sure that we even began to advertise for staff but one difficulty after another cropped up and it began to look as though we might have to postpone opening for a very long time. But since I began to write this Report we have heard from the Ministry of Education that they will be able to make us an Accommodation Grant of £15,000. This will enable us to go ahead with our plans…I hope that we shall have Mr W David Wills and his wife to run the School as Warden and House Mother.

The work at Bodenham will be an attempt to make permanent the work which Mr Wills did at Barnes in Scotland. All of the experimental work was done there and it was proved that delinquency can be prevented, and I believe entirely wiped out, by his methods….£32,000 may seem a very large amount of money for a small number of children but I want to emphasise over and over again that this is a vital experiment which I believe is going to affect the welfare of children all over England and the capital sum must be looked on in the same way as if it were hospital equipment. The cost of our hospitals for physical ill health is very high, and rightly so, but the cost of the necessity of achieving mental health is not so widely recognised…."

Privately, in a letter to Hilda dated July 1947, he shows his frustration:

"Ogwen Lake Cottage

…I can't make much of the Trust Deed ((The Ministry had required the School to be set up under an educational trust)) and it strikes me that most of it is purely formal and would be a dead letter for the most part but H B Hurrell does not seem such a damnable stick as Bosworth Smith. He writes as 'Dear Mr Mathews'. I think it can stand over till you and I and perhaps David and Mr Austin can talk it over…Some of it does not fit with our scheme as it does not provide for a Warden and it does provide for Religious Education which David does not give, at least he did not at Barnes. …

You will find out from David what his reactions are to having 5 or 6 children but when I saw Burns … he thought that the Education

Committee would send us children. This involves an interview with someone …. I am not at all sure it is sane or wise to have children while the alterations are going on. The suggestion I made at last Committee was one made in despair thinking we should go on and on negotiating with Bosworth Smith. …"

Frank's enthusiasm for the new venture did not deflect him from what had been the core business of the Society since it started – the country boarding out of "nervous" children. In fact, the 1947 - 48 Report starts with a discussion of boarding out illustrated, as was Frank's habit, by stories about some of the children:

"…For the moment I want those who have helped us so much with money and interest ((to know)) that, to my mind, the last two years of the Society's work have been the most fruitful of all. In the boarding out there is a more complete understanding of the difficulties of the children by the foster mothers which has added very greatly to the results that we have been able to obtain. Of course we have had some failures but we have had many results which have more than repaid all the money and time spent on them. This is in spite of the fact that in the country, and remote as these children often are, it is impossible to get regular psychiatric help.

Also it is noteworthy that during these last two years no child has run away, though on one occasion two children disappeared on an October morning at 10. am for an impromptu adventure, lost their way and returned at 8 the next morning. One of the girls was just thirteen, the other about nine, and with no food, but two adventure stories, they decided to camp out for the day. They lost their way and had to sleep out for the night. They returned very weary and bedraggled and the little one remarked, with a sigh, 'Its better here'. It speaks volumes for the foster mother in question in that our advice was strictly adhered to – neither child was asked where she had been, what she had done or why she had gone, and life in the little farm went on as though nothing had happened, apart from hot mustard baths and warm beds for the strain on the foster mother, to say nothing of ourselves and the children's own parents.

I suppose our most outstanding success has been that of a girl of fifteen who was sent to us by the Provisional Council for Mental Health. She had had chorea almost continuously since she was four and a half and had been treated in hospital after hospital for short periods but, as I have always found in these cases of chronic chorea, nothing but temporary cures were obtained. At first she had no belief at all – in fact one might say she had an anti-belief – that she would get well. Fretful, miserable, shaking almost like an aspen at times and quite sure that her heart was affected, this girl came to us, but after a month or two the foster mother, unknown to her saw her vault a five barred gate….At the end of eighteen months she began to get restless and wanted, of all occupations to be a nurse…..we were able to arrange for her to go to a little country hospital where the work was reasonably hard though not beyond her capacity. This has been a great success….

An interesting sidelight on our work in this case was that, on visiting the home in the absence of this girl we found a sister of twelve years in a somewhat emaciated condition with spinal curvature. She was going to hospital for treatment but her general physical condition was so poor that the treatment was not having any measure of success. We sent her to another little farm in the country for six months and at the end of that time she returned home, re-started her treatment with results that have been miraculous….I mention this because it has always been our rule to visit the family rather than just the one child….

Another little girl who shows great promise was also sent to us as being unmanageable. She has been boarded out for eighteen months. At first her sulky fits were so violent that she would sit for long periods with her head on the table and could not be roused even by the utmost patience. She was so difficult that I was asked by the foster mother, or rather father, to send her home at once as, he said, all the time they had had children (which was about twenty years) they had not had one as bad as this. We laid low about this request as we knew the child was very happy there, and in three weeks we received a letter from the foster mother saying that they wished to keep her. Now, a few months later, she has grown into a lively bright little girl who no longer dawdles to school, and when we visit bounds over the fields to meet us….

A large proportion of the children who come to us are not like these and are apt to be looked upon as nothing more than delinquent, but I do know that at some time or another they have undergone some strain which was greater than their nervous system could bear. We know, too, that difficult children are very often the products of a disturbed or broken home – nearly always one or other of the parents has had similar conditions in childhood – and I came to the conclusion that much more intensive work was needed to help the parents. About eighteen months ago we appointed as Secretary Mrs H A Rees who had for many years given us very valuable voluntary part time help, and are now able to do what I have long wanted to do – that is, long personal visits. We find that many, if not most, of the parents have had early lives of some difficulty and are carrying burdens of responsibility and fear almost beyond their capacity to bear, but many women, and men also, can be encouraged to discuss their difficulties, their fears and anxieties, with someone in whom they have confidence that they will be understood....

We feel that it is not enough just to send a child away and return it to the same environment as things might go wrong again, but if, while the child is away, and, of equal importance, for long after it has returned home, visits are frequent enough to inspire confidence and the security of understanding and friendship then the whole attitude of the parents can be changed and the child's cure can be made permanent..."

This was to be Frank's last annual report. When he wrote it, toward the end of 1947, he was within a few weeks of becoming bedridden with his final illness. But it still shows him looking forward and still very much at the helm.

But to go back to 1945; at about the time of Frank's first visit to the Ministry of Education he was able to appoint a social worker, as he had intended, to help with the home visiting. For some reason the appointment was not satisfactory and it was ended in July 1946. This left Frank with the task of finding a replacement and he knew that he would have difficulty in finding someone both trained and experienced in social work and in full sympathy with his ideas. He must have decided to give the sympathy first priority and hope that Hilda both would and could do the social work in addition to running the day to day business of the Society.

She had no formal training in social work though she was fully competent to look after the day to day business. Even more worrying from her point of view, she had two young children and a home to look after. Although the money would be more than welcome the sheer physical effort of housekeeping was much greater in the 1940s. The idea of plunging into social work may have worried her – though it was not her openly expressed concern at the time – but when Frank asked her to take on the dual role of Secretary of the Society and social worker, both, initially in support of himself, after consulting her family, she decided to accept his offer.

Following her appointment in 1946 Hilda took over most of the family visiting which by then was for both "invalid" and "nervous" children. Her notes of the visits between October of that year and May of 1948 provide a detailed and striking picture of the wide range of problems faced by the children and their families and of what was being done to help them.

During that period she made two hundred and eighty home visits to seventy families. Some were to newly referred children, some were to the families of children who were away and some were to the families of children who had been away. At the beginning of the period Frank was also visiting children who were subsequently transferred to her list.

Typically, families would be visited every two or three months while children were away, monthly for a few months after their return and then three monthly for several years. The visits would be used to hear and report progress, to listen to family problems and offer advice and help and to supply vitamins and dietary supplements for family members needing them.

The notes show clearly that even when only one member of a family might be judged to need to go away others would often be in need of support in one form or another. A few examples will give some idea of the variety of problems and of the help offered:

'C' was a delicate little girl with a speech defect: she was three years old when first seen. The notes give no indication of behavioural difficulty though both C and her mother were worried by the speech problem. Virol (a dietary supplement) was provided for C and vitamins for her mother. The parents were persuaded to allow C to go for three months to a convalescent hospital where she was happy and gained weight. They were unable to bring themselves to allow the stay to be extended and there was some temporary regression when C returned home. Medical opinion was that the speech defect was structural but the parents were advised to wait until C was five before doing anything about it. Two other children seemed to have no particular problems and Hilda considered the family to be normal.

'A' was boarded out for a year when he was ten having been referred by Dr Burns for temper fits and fighting with loss of control. He did well while away but was fetched home, prematurely, it was thought, and still boisterous. By the time this happened visits to the family had started to reveal serious tensions between the parents which became worse in the succeeding months, the father attacking the mother through the children and particularly through A who he hit frequently.

The family had some financial problems stemming from intermittent employment: agreed payments toward A's boarding out were reduced at one stage. A seems to have been physically strong but his mother and at least one of his sisters were not, the mother having needed surgery for back problems. They were helped with dietary supplements.

Hilda visited the family nine times in the nine months after A's return home from boarding out. There was at least one visit to the child guidance clinic and other agencies, including the NSPCC, were called in as the family situation moved toward separation. She noted that, despite all the family problems, A seemed to cope well, even adopting a philosophical attitude to his father's violence. Hilda felt that he, at least, was progressing toward an outcome that would be acceptable to him.

'M' was referred by the Child Guidance Clinic, aged twelve. She was difficult to manage at home, was jealous of her older brother and younger sister and stole things for no obvious reason. She was boarded out for almost two years, and was very happy in her foster home. Her pilfering continued while she was there but was never linked with any particular upset. She enjoyed the countryside and would have liked to work there but no job could be found.

Back in Birmingham she found work in a children's nursery where she seemed happy. Her home life was turbulent: she ate poorly, her parents described her as stupid, boorish and ill mannered. Outside the home she behaved well socially and seemed bright. The matron of her nursery dealt sympathetically with her pilfering and follow up psychiatric help was arranged.

During the months following M's return Hilda visited frequently and contact was kept up with the foster parents by letters and visits. Early on Hilda formed the opinion that M's problems were too severe to be helped by what the Society could do. Nevertheless, support was continued and by the time she was nineteen years old M was reported to be working in a hospital and to be happy in her work, making friends of her own sex and to be acquiring an easier manner with both adults and contemporaries. Difficulties at home persisted but Hilda felt that M was on her way to a reasonably satisfactory adjustment.

* * *

In 1947 an appeal was launched by the Society to commemorate Frank's fifty years service in social work for children. The appeal, signed by Harold Austin, Chairman of the Society, outlined Frank's work and achievements up to the purchase of Bodenham Manor and asked for £5,000 to complete the alterations and equipment, it being estimated that this would be what was required on top of the money the Society already had and what had been promised by the Ministry of Education.

The appeal appears to have been Frank's idea. He would have been unlikely to have missed such an obvious opportunity for fund raising and he certainly discussed it in detail with Hilda in July:

"… tho' its very difficult for me to suggest it is to exploit the fact that on the first of April next it will be exactly 50 years since I started the Cripples Hospital (Cripples Union really) and that I have been doing social work of some value to the City for 50 years and they would like to commemorate this by raising £1,000 or £1,500 …"

Someone, clearly, decided to use the higher figure of £5,000 and by the end of the 1947 – 48 financial year £1,765 had been raised for the Country School fund with more to come from covenanted subscriptions. Income to the school fund in that year was £3,378, including £1,002 from the calendars and £416 from the Society's general fund. The ongoing expenditure that had worried Frank after David Wills' early appointment was £1080 leaving the balance of £2,297 to be put toward capital expenditure. The following year the School fund had a surplus of £1,660 and the gap in capital provision was more or less closed.

In September 1947 Frank took a holiday in Dolgelly on the slopes of Cader Idris, the mountain he had climbed on his first holidays at Barmouth more than fifty years before. He wrote to Hilda on the 18th:

"….I want to put on paper too what I have said to you many times, but never too many times, what a joy and pleasure your coming on the permanent staff has been and is to me. Never in my working life have I worked in such entire harmony with anyone, a harmony so real and perfect that I could not have imagined possible, the more wonderful too with the disparity in our ages. I hope, I earnestly hope, I am not a trial to you. If at any time you do find me difficult you have only to say and the difficulty will be moved at once. …

The holiday here has been a surprise. On Monday I planned a 14 or 15 mile walk… but found myself so fagged I had to give up the idea of long walks, 4 or 5 miles and that was quite enough. Tuesday … I started out at 2 o'clock for a stroll and finished up doing about 9 miles over the precipice walk which I'd not seen for 20 years and found it as lovely as ever and found myself quite fresh when I got here.

So today I went up Cader by a …path which I had never been on before, did 6 hours walking on 5 small handfuls of dried raisins and came down a way I'd not have chosen … missed the track, never saw it till I got within 20 minutes of the bottom … feel entirely renewed. I created a small sensation at the top as there were two members of the Rock and Fell Club in the tea hut, one said 'well if I could do a climb like that at 76 I've got another 20 years'.

But I'm having cramp and expect some more when I go to bed, but it was a wonderful day …

I'm disappointed with this letter. I have not said all I feel about you or expressed adequately the joy and pleasure and help your coming to the office has brought me.

With my grateful love to you

Yours always, FM"

This seems to be the last letter Frank wrote to Hilda. It was not his last holiday: there is a reference to one that he took in January 1948, but it is probably the last time he was fit enough for the kind of climbing he had loved for so long so the letter is probably, as it reads, valedictory in two senses.

On Wednesday 2nd June 1948 Frank announced the financial backing from the Ministry of Education that had made it possible to proceed with the opening of Bodenham Manor School. He described the proposal to a reporter from the Birmingham Gazette who commented the next day on his enthusiasm, remarking that Frank had been bedridden for the previous six months. The next morning he became unconscious. He died on the Saturday, the 6th June

Although his last illness was painful – after a lifetime of principled abstinence he had to dull the pain with sips of brandy – he continued to work right to the end though the induced depression sometimes brought about self doubt. Once, in the last few days he said to Hilda "I have ploughed sand".

By contrast, the Birmingham Gazette's article announcing Frank's death included a quotation from a letter received in response to the Thursday article:

> "I am one of the lame children who benefited by his work nearly fifty years ago, and I should like to thank him for what he has done for me"

The memorial card prepared for Frank's funeral contained no religious references, simply his name, address and dates and, inside, some lines that he had written in his notebook and quoted on a number of occasions:

> "Better than martial woe
> Or the pageant of civic sorrow,
>
> Better than the praise of today
> Or the Statue we build tomorrow,
>
> Better than honour or glory'
> Or History's iron pen,
>
> Is the thought of duty done,
> And the love of our fellow men.

AFTERWARDS

Hilda took charge of the business of the Society. In addition to the routine of meetings and fundraising she became correspondent with the Ministry of Education. She continued the home visiting and also took on responsibility for visits to boarded out children.

Frank left his car to the Society and Hilda had to learn to drive it rather suddenly so that the visiting could be continued. Despite never having driven anything she had held a full license for all imaginable vehicles since Leslie bought his first motor cycle. Her first license had been issued in the early 1930s, when there was no such thing as a driving test, and she had never actually got round even to driving the cycle. That license had long since lapsed, but, under the law as it was in 1948, the authorities were obliged to issue a new license without question. Fortunately, she quickly became proficient and drove for the rest of her life without accident.

Evelyn became Honorary Secretary and continued to be active in the Society for the rest of her long life. As well as serving on its various committees she took part in the fundraising activities which continued unabated, including the annual distribution of calendars from 47 Maple Road. She usually went with Hilda to visit boarded out children. Gwen Hazelwood continued as Assistant Secretary and Myra Wynn Thomas was among those who continued to help in the office.

For a time, boarding out and its associated home visiting continued to be the main activity.

The records show that 400 children were fostered in the twenty one years between 1937 and 1958 and another 120 spent periods, usually of the order of three months, in country hospitals and convalescent homes. A small proportion of children returned home within a few days. Between 1937 and 1955 three hundred and seven children were fostered for periods ranging from a month or two to several years. Two thirds of them were boarded out for a year or less and the remainder for up to five years. 27 stayed away for more than two years, a few electing to remain permanently in their foster homes.

There were, altogether, twenty seven foster homes. Some of these were inherited from the former Invalid Children's Society. Others come from recommendations from local people including clergy, schoolteachers and existing carers. Some foster parents took only one or two children and were involved for a relatively short time but ten took at least ten children each over periods of five years or more. Rosa and Mabel Price were among the foster parents inherited from the Invalid Children's Society. Rosa continued until boarding out finished in 1958 the sisters taking 99 girls and 2 boys between November 1937 and April 1958 on their smallholding on Wenlock Edge. Mrs Griffiths of Bitterley was also involved from start to finish, taking 46 girls between 1938 and 1957 and Miss N Edwards fostered 46 boys between 1947 and 1952.

Hilda's notebook of visits during 1956, when boarding out was starting to wind down, shows that she, or the Society's social worker, made a round of foster homes, every two weeks on average. In that year three new foster parents were recruited and eight homes and seventeen children were being visited. Nevertheless, as the Society's 1969 Annual Report records, the call for boarding out had become progressively less over the years as more provision was made by local authorities and statutory bodies, and the Society brought this aspect of its work to an end in April 1958 at which point Hilda gave up paid work and became Honorary Secretary of the Society, Evelyn becoming a Vice President.

Some children did not seem to be helped by the foster care. Others relapsed when they returned to their parents. But there is evidence that boarding out did have many successes even with the children with persistent behavioural problems who, Frank thought, needed the more skilled care that could be provided in a residential school.

Some time, probably in 1943, he commented in the Society's boarding out register on the outcome of completed treatments. The comments are terse but it seems, for example, that of 37 children who had spent some time away during the financial year 1940-41 he considered that the outcome was satisfactory in 22 cases and that there were 6 failures, three of the children having gone on to approved school.

In a forward to the Society's 1948-49 Annual Report Dr Burns reports on an analysis of a follow up of about a hundred children he had recommended for boarding out. He divides them into those children whose problems were "nervous" and those exhibiting challenging behaviour. Though his judgements were necessarily subjective, the analysis shows clearly that some of those with challenging behaviour did get better but that children of the nervous type had been much more likely to be helped by being boarded out.

But there does not seem to have been any more sustained attempt at a systematic follow up of the treatment: even now, an effort to do so might not be wasted.

It was, after all, very cheap. For example, The Society's accounts for 1940-41 show a total expenditure of £1146 of which £768 was spent on farm boarding out, £44 on medicines and special foods, £143 on office salaries and £5 depreciation of office furniture and equipment. Income was £1349 of which £191 came from parents' payments, almost all the rest having been raised by charitable activities. The 37 children treated in that year spent a total of 233 months away at an average cost of £5 per month, probably about a third of the average monthly wage at the time.

In the early days of the Society conditions in the city were very harsh for poor people. During the war years from 1939 to 1945 plentiful jobs and the price control and rationing of food improved some of the economic conditions but families were split by war service, houses, especially in the inner city, were often damaged and people had at times to endure the stresses of being bombed. After the war improvement of physical conditions did not really gather pace until the 1950s.

It is hardly surprising in these circumstances that a comparatively simple form of therapy appears to have been successful in many cases. Physical conditions in the country were not necessarily all that much better than in the city. Most houses would have had no mains services, public transport was sparse and country wages were even lower than those in town. But country life was adapted to those conditions and the money paid to foster parents, small though it was, helped to ease life in their homes.

Much of the success of the boarding out may have been due simply to the children concerned being kept in such a safe and unstressed environment and otherwise supported until they had time to grow out of their difficulties. But whether or not this was so, there is no doubt that the support given to both the children and their families helped them a great deal at the time. Many of the bonds formed lasted for decades after the treatment had ended: some, perhaps, endure today.

* * *

Bodenham Manor School finally opened in March 1950 with David Wills as Warden. It was recognised by the Ministry of Education as a residential school of 30 places for maladjusted boys up to the age of eleven and girls up to the school leaving age. . Hilda continued to supervise the office side of the case work for both boarded out and Bodenham children, sometimes visiting parents at home, sometimes seeing them at the office, but it soon became clear that help was needed and efforts were made to recruit a social worker. The first of several qualified people was recruited in 1951.

Naturally, the school was visited by the civil servants, who seem to have been bemused, and the local Schools Medical Officer at their request. The first visit by an inspector was made on 23rd November 1950. She found minor teething problems but came to a generally favourable conclusion:

". …. The Manor, formerly occupied by one of the Arkwright family, has been well adapted for the purpose of a residential school. The equipment is good but more has yet to be supplied; the playrooms are still bare.

The Staff consists of the Warden (Mr. David Wills) and a House Mother (Mrs. Wills) a Matron (untrained, formerly a nurse), an assistant Matron (does the work of a maid), two men cooks, a handyman (a graduate of Edinburgh) and a gardener.

Daily Staff: three part-time cleaners.

The Teaching Staff consists of:

Mr. H.J. Slade, a qualified assistant master (E.T.C. Watford) appointed Easter 1950.

A trainee without any qualification, who is serving a year here to gain experience before taking up a course of study in social science.

N.B. The Head Mistress, in charge of the School from its opening, left last term. The Warden did not consider she was suitable for this work.

At the time of this visit Mr. Slade, a teacher in his probationary period, had charge of the School. (It is necessary for a Head Teacher to be appointed without delay if the strain is not to prove too heavy for the assistant teacher here)….

…. There were 26 pupils resident. The age range was from 7 to 11 years; they had all been sent to the School by L.E.A.s and the charge per child was £250 (yearly).

The I.Q. level - this was from 76 to 131.

Holidays

The pupils go home for a week three times a year. This year the staff and pupils were remaining at School for the Christmas holiday, including Christmas Day.

Eneuretics   Of the 26 pupils in the School, nine were eneuretic.

Speech defects   One pupil was noticed to stammer.

… The pupils appear to be happy, well cared for, and on good terms with the staff, whose Christian names are used by the children. All the staff share the responsibility for the well-being of the children, and each adult is in charge of a small group of them. The children are shown interest and given affection to which they respond. The teacher-in-charge is successful in his handling of them; there are domestic pets such as a dog and rabbits and a number of the children have their own cats.

Staff accommodation … is adequate. …The resident staff have a day off duty weekly; they work extremely hard and their day with the children is long. Many of the girls do not go off to sleep until 8.30 - 9.0 p.m. … It is sacrificial work and the staff seem happy carrying out their duties. The School shows promise. … It is expected that the shortest length of stay will be 6 months, but some pupils will probably need longer treatment over a period of several years.

… The children have a measure of self-government; their Chairman, a girl of eleven, calls upon one of them to say grace before meals. At the end of dinner she asks if there are any 'notices'; the Warden, several children, and H.M.I. accepted this invitation to say a few words. The 'Chairman' then dismissed the children. The staff appear to have everything in common and they use Christian names to address each other. All the resident staff, including the cooks, eat at the tables with the children, and at the mid-morning break and after dinner when a pot of tea is served in the staff-room, the staff meet together as friends. The handyman (a graduate) is successful in handling the boys out of school and they delight to help him in his duties; he is a trained teacher as is assistant Matron. There are indeed three trained and qualified teachers on the staff; the Warden is not a teacher. The children are shown a great deal of kindness and there is no doubt that all the staff are actuated by high ideals. It is too soon to come to any conclusions but the children appear to be happy and are sympathetically handled.

I left this School at 3.00 p.m. and paid a visit to another School in the village. On my return journey from the village past the School I met all of the children with several members of the staff, including the Warden, taking a walk before tea. One child had a birthday and I had found her earlier in with the Warden arranging the games to be played after tea at her birthday. The cooks had made an iced birthday cake and I learned from the children that they always had a party if anyone had a birthday. There seems a great deal ... kindness in this place and the children seem to respond to it."

The school was established under a trust, later registered as a charity, that was governed by a committee of managers, mostly appointed by the Society. The fees, paid by local authorities, were set at a level that made the school essentially self supporting though the Society would pay for extras and improvements.

Although the fees were thought to be relatively high the school was full almost from the start and remained so. For example, in 1959 there were 58 applications for admission of children from all over the country. Only 10 could be accepted: 5 came from Birmingham, 2 from Coventry and one each from Essex, Northamptonshire and the West Riding of Yorkshire. The school seems to have been well regarded by professionals and the Ministry was, generally, very supportive.

In 1957 the accommodation was enlarged by the addition of a teacher's flat and staff room, the cost being born by a grant from the Birmingham University Carnival fund supplemented by additional funds from the Ministry. This released some extra room for children so their number was increased to 32, but because of difficulties encountered in discharging boys at the age of 11 it was decided to change to a single sex school, the last remaining girls being discharged in July 1958.

There was a general concern, expressed especially by David Wills, about what would happen to boys when they became too old to stay at the school. An attempt to tackle this problem was made in

1959-60 when the Society bought The Dell, a house in Malvern, which needed little conversion to make it into a hostel for 12 adolescent boys, the intention being that it would provide follow on treatment after Bodenham Manor School and would work in conjunction with the School.

When the hostel was opened there were no boys at Bodenham ready for transfer though there were plenty of applications from elsewhere. Unfortunately, though, the distance from Bodenham was great enough to prevent the close interworking that had been hoped for and, furthermore, it proved very difficult to recruit and retain staff. By 1965 it had become clear that the arrangements were unsustainable and the Society decided to bring them to an end.

Nevertheless, it was still felt that there was a need and, learning from the experience at The Dell, the Society bought a smaller house, The Laurels, at Marden only a few miles from the School. This was treated as an annexe to the school with boys who had moved there being under the immediate care of a housefather and housemother and still being able to attend the school if need be. Alternatively, they could go to the local secondary modern school or go out to work. Thus the capacity was effectively increased by six places and the possible age range extended.

In 1961, much to Hilda's and the managers', regret David Wills decided to leave. The post of Warden had been created solely so that Wills could lead the school and, with his departure, there was no need to retain it. It was decided, therefore, to go over to the Ministry's preferred structure with overall responsibility vested in a Headmaster. This post was occupied until 1965 by R D Bilbey and after that by E R Saunders.

The School continued to develop and early in 1969 four new classrooms and two staff bungalows were built, three quarters of the cost being met by the Ministry and a quarter by the Society using money from legacies.

In June of that year Evelyn Mathews died at the age of 92. Gwen, now married to Arthur Hallsworth, had taken over the tenancy of 23 Laburnum Road on the death of Mrs Wheelwright in 1960 and had thus become the Society's landlady. She died a year later aged only 61. She was succeeded as Assistant Secretary by Mary Birks who had worked in the office since 1949.

Meanwhile Hilda had been broadening her interests much as Frank had predicted and urged. In March 1958 she was appointed a Justice of the Peace for Birmingham on the nomination of her local Labour Party. She was by then too old to be put on the Juvenile Panel, for which her experience would have been ideal, but she served on the main bench until she moved from the City almost 20 years later.

In 1964 she was co-opted to the Birmingham Education Committee and served on that Committee special services sub-committee and was a West District School Manager for three years. After this she continued to represent the Committee on the boards of three voluntary schools and by 1969 had become a member of the North District Special Schools Committee. In 1970 she was appointed MBE.

In 1972 when she passed her 65th birthday Hilda told her fellow committee members that she felt it was time for her to retire. She had, by that time, led the work of the Society for 24 years, first as Secretary, then as Honorary Secretary and Vice President, and had overseen improvements in the facilities at Bodenham Manor School, the opening and closing of the hostel at The Dell and the opening of The Laurels at Marden. But there were, by 1972, no proposals for major new initiatives and it is not surprising that her decision to step down set off discussions about the future of the Society and of Bodenham Manor School. These led, in 1975, to a formal decision to wind up the Society which, as the Honorary Solicitor (G Corbyn Barrow) put it, apart from receiving funds, which continued to accumulate, had become virtually an appointing committee for managers of the school.

At the final General Meeting of the Society in September 1975 he reported that the Committee would have liked to hand over the running of the school to the Birmingham local authority, this being seen as the best way to ensure its continuation. The school was itself a charity and its assets were, therefore, vested in the Charity Commissioners so, whatever the arrangement it would remain a separate entity. The City authorities were known to be interested in taking over its management.

The winding up of the Society and the pursuit of a suitable arrangement for the school were agreed by the meeting though it was another two or three years before arrangements could be concluded and the running of the school handed over to the City. Meanwhile, substantial amounts of money had continued to accumulate, largely in the form of legacies from long time supporters. The problem of what to do with this was solved by forming a new Bodenham Amenities Trust, an independent charity.

The last Statement of Accounts, issued at the end of 1979 records that the investments transferred to the Bodenham Amenities Trust were Treasury Stock 7¾% - 2012/15 to the nominal value of £23,300 and that:

> "The last meeting of the Committee of the Birmingham Society for the Care of Invalid and Nervous Children was held on 14 September 1977 and the accounts were finally closed on audit 28th November 1978, the transfer of the investments being made from the present Trustees to the new ones and the deed being dated and signed on 18th April 1978."

The school continued under a Board of Governors appointed by the Birmingham Education Committee until 1987 when the governors decided, somewhat controversially, to close it. The school was closed at the end of the summer term of that year, the charity which owned the capital assets, Bodenham Manor School itself, being renamed the "Birmingham Bodenham Trust". The income from the assets is used to help children with a range of handicaps.

POST SCRIPT

Frank Mathews spent his working life helping children and was, in his time, known and loved by thousands of people. He was well respected by influential people in Birmingham and elsewhere and was, although he had no formal training, well thought of by professionals in the fields in which he worked.

It has not been to difficult to reconstruct the story of his work from the published records of the charities that he founded and ran but he kept only a small collection of key documents about himself – sufficient to give a general idea of his personal history and interests but with tantalising gaps, some of which I have not been able to fill. Fortunately a series of about sixty letters written to my mother were kept and provide, along with her recorded recollections, a window into his private self.

Thus, one way or another, it has been possible to put together a reasonably balanced, even if incomplete, account of his thoughts and deeds.

* * *

An outsider's view of the quality of Frank's work was given shortly after his death by Clair Britton who was, at the time, training boarding out officers in London. She had recently visited some of the foster homes used by his Society at the time:

> "…I tried to understand the important things about what I saw and heard, and it seems to me that of the first importance is the fact that you have never allowed yourself to deal with numbers but have kept the work within your own compass, and therefore preserved its intimate and personal nature. I do see that this is

fundamental to good foster home placement, for needs are essentially personal, and must be felt as such if real help is to be given. Then following on from that the care and trouble you have taken to establish and preserve your relationships is a very important part of the work, for it must give a sense of continuity and stability to foster parents and children alike. The way in which you look after the foster mothers as well as the children impressed me, and the contact which is maintained throughout with the child's home seems a very necessary part of the work – but I have never heard of it being done by anyone else….

…The whole experience reinforced what I already felt – that we must fight hard to keep the work small, within the compass of the individual worker – for only then can the necessary care and thought be put into it – and without this no very fundamental change can be brought about in the lives of the children. For if nobody is deeply concerned and taking a lot of trouble – then nothing happens!…"

The letter picks out many of the things that Frank himself had considered to be vital to his success – particularly the continuity, the provision of long term follow up and support of the children and their families and, above all the personal relationships possible when working on a small scale. This, combined with the long after care that he insisted on, may well have been his greatest innovation in treatment methods

No exact record has survived, but the total number of children helped by the Invalid and Nervous Children's Societies must have been well in excess of a thousand to add to, perhaps, ten thousand helped by the Cripples Union.

* * *

Frank would have been the first to point out that he could not have done what he did without devoted help but it was one of his talents that he could inspire people to give him that help, often over very many years.

His most devoted helper, over their more than forty years of marriage, was Evelyn. She had shown and developed her artistic talent before they were married and could readily have made a career, and perhaps have achieved fame, as a book illustrator. But she seems to have given all that up completely to help him, as a volunteer officer in the Cripples Union, as a member of the Ivy Fellowship, as Chairman of the Women's Guild and in countless aspects of the day to day working of his charities.

Frank wrote several times to Hilda of his contentment with his marriage. It does seem to have been happy, but perhaps he mentioned it more times than might have been expected. Also, he expressed, more than once, his discomfort in the presence of very small children and it is tempting to suggest that their absence in his life meant more to him than he was prepared to say and that the lack of a sexual side to his marriage, which he admitted privately to her, was a cause of real sadness to him. However, if so, it was compensated for, to a great extent, by the warm companionship that existed between Frank and Evelyn throughout their time together.

It may be that the delicacy Arthur Holden saw in his daughter had as much to do with her feelings as with any physical symptoms and that the delicacy, and even the ill health, were symptoms of a lack of emotional robustness – something that Evelyn's later life suggests she may eventually have overcome. If so, this may provide some sort of explanation for any lack of physical contact in her relationship with Frank.

When he was a young man Frank's mother must have wondered what more she could do for a son who could not settle for a normal job in an office and was neither enthusiastic about a career in horticulture nor motivated to make a success in trade. She would have seen his enthusiasm for his work with the Cinderella Club and might have believed that he had found his metier at the Hurst Street Mission but, sadly, she died before his life's work really got under way. Frank said that his mother had taken to drink in her later years, and no wonder if she had after a hard life, but too much weight should not, perhaps be given to the opinion of a lifelong abstainer as to what constitutes "taking to drink".

Frank maintained friendship with, and was also able to inspire long term loyalty in, people with whom he did not have family ties. The work of Albert Wort as Secretary for over forty years of the Workman's Auxiliary Committee has been mentioned.

Others who stayed with Frank for many years included Myra Wynn Thomas, originally recruited as a home crafts teacher for the Cripples Union at the turn of the century, Ann Davies and Florrie West, once a patient and later an administrator of the Cripples Union. They were among those who worked regularly in the office, writing out personal appeal letters from which much of the regular income of the Nervous Children's Society derived. All three served on Frank's committees. Frank's long friendship with Hilda was the foundation of the continuation of his work for "nervous" children long after his death. She was supported by Gwen Hallsworth (Hazelwood) and, of course, by Evelyn, for the rest of their lives.

* * *

Frank's accomplishment as a worker and as an inspirational leader are, then, beyond doubt but what sort of a man was he?

Physically he was impressive. He was six feet tall, he was always well dressed and he had an unassuming self confidence that allowed him to be equally at ease in any company. Because of his deafness his voice was not well controlled and this sometimes frightened people at first though his kindness, particularly to vulnerable people, soon dispelled their fears. He spoke to children as though they were human and they liked him.

His and Evelyn's requirements were modest. He worked for many years for a salary that was less, even, than those of many charity workers with less demanding jobs. When he and Evelyn inherited enough money to live on he no longer took either wage or honorarium. Their home was small and sparsely furnished and they did not own it. For much of the time they allowed part of it to be used for Frank's work.

What money they did have was, however, spent in a way that reflected their class and upbringing. They had domestic help, they wore clothes of good quality, they took frequent holidays and they had a middle class car – a Wolseley – though a reliable car was a necessity for the work and the holidays were, without a doubt, needed as a relief from the tiredness that came, increasingly, from the pace of Frank's work.

Mentally, Frank appears, on the surface, to have been a mass of contradictions. His philosophy of life, derived from his wide reading, was based on a combination of socialism, pacifism and the most tolerant of religious teaching. As such it was consistent and defensible but he seems to have combined with it credulity about magic of various sorts from palmistry to spiritualism. His attitude to human suffering, especially among children, was entirely compassionate but he seems to have viewed its amelioration completely dispassionately: if he came across a child his reason told him he could not help he stopped trying. The thrust that he applied to his work seemed unstoppable but he took the trouble to evaluate his results in an essentially scientific fashion - though he had no scientific education - and adjusted his methods accordingly.

All in all, the best that can be said is that his contradictions, such as they were, seem to have had little, if any, effect on his work however much they may have exercised his thoughts.

* * *

Frank admitted to having a temper which he claimed to have got under some control as he got older. It seemed to be roused by frustrations of all kinds. The telephone, particularly, often offended him because he would misunderstand things said over it. Once, for example, he attempted to ring a senior executive in a firm that donated to the Society only to bang the receiver down with a complaint the "they" had connected him to the bloody zoo now. He had, presumably, forgotten that the firm was Kalamazoo, a well known office supplies manufacturer. He did swear quite a bit in an old fashioned sort of way.

But his real ill feeling was reserved for bureaucracy when it got in his way. He was always clear in his own mind about what he wanted to achieve – he couldn't possibly have achieved what he did without that clarity and the directness of action that stemmed from it.

When he started his work his style was completely appropriate. There was very little in the way of state apparatus: what was done over a wide range of health care was done by private initiative with charitable support. Anyone who was prepared to take the responsibility of doing something was, gratefully, allowed to do it. As time went on society gradually caught up with the multiplicity of needs for social action and the field ceased to be so clear. By the time Frank started the Invalid Children's society there were several organisations doing related work and he had, at one point, to correct in print any suggestion that he thought he was working alone. The Nervous Children's Society was a truly pioneering venture when he started it but by the time he was ready to open his school a whole raft of social legislation had come about and he had to negotiate his way through all sorts of new influences.

Negotiation of this kind was not his strongest point and he undoubtedly found it very frustrating to have to take on endless committees and meetings with officials. But he had to try to suppress his frustration. There seems little doubt that it was at the back of much of the physical ill health that he referred to in his letters. Fortunately in his last years he had help with the negotiation from people who were good at it.

Despite his youthful poor health he must have been constitutionally strong to do as much as he did into middle age and to carry on working until his mid seventies. He did have problems with his back but they came and went in rhythm, it seemed, with the mental stresses of his work

It was obvious to everyone that he was passionate about his work but his passion also extended to other sides of his life. He loved reading and listening to classical music and gained great pleasure for many years from touring by motor cycle and car. But, above all, he loved mountains and delighted in roaming over them, even until his last months and it was in this activity above all that he found the cure for the tensions that built up while he was working. He said, in later life, that he actually preferred to be in the mountains on his own, often in circumstances that conventional wisdom would have considered risky if not downright dangerous.

This communing with mountains was one of the key aspects of his spiritual life and one that came to him without being consciously sought. It is clear from his carefully recorded reading that even in his teens he was not satisfied with the conventional Christianity of his childhood and that he was looking for a creed to live by that somehow took in both the teachings of religion and of secular philosophy. But in the end his religion and philosophy were, to him, rationalisations of what he was and what he did.

He was not always consistent about his rationalisation. He claimed to believe in the supremacy of reason, but in the end achieved what he did because of passion – surely no reasonable person would have tried. He was not particularly good at seeing the other side of arguments, especially when confronted by bureaucracy. He told Hilda off when he decided that she was not conducting her life according to a plan but it is hard to make out the point at which he might have formulated one of his own.

But he was completely single minded and consistent about the way he conducted his adult life, planned or not. He was a deeply compassionate man who could not contemplate suffering without wanting to do something about it. He could not address all the suffering in the world directly and he didn't want to try to improve the world by political means. He was content to leave that to others, though he followed what they did and spoke out when he thought it was wrong.

* * *

Frank was who he was and accomplished what he did through a combination of energy and passion. His own early history gives us a clue to the origin of his passion, or compassion, for relieving the sufferings of children but where did he get the energy?

Part of the explanation must lie in the contentment with which he and Evelyn conducted their life together.

After his father's early death Frank's mother worked to make it possible to maintain middle class standards and she had help from her own reasonably affluent parents. Frank and his brother had good educations by the standards of the time. Nevertheless, by the time he reached manhood, Frank was well used to being comfortable while having not much money.

Although the Holdens, by contrast, were well off and always lived in large comfortable houses they were by no means ostentatious and their style of living was simple. The family were mainly interested in cultural pursuits. The acquisition and spending of money did not in any way dominate their every day lives.

Thus, when Frank and Evelyn married they were easily satisfied with a modest and inexpensive house furnished in an aesthetically pleasing but inexpensive way. The money available to them was enough for their needs and they never, even though they were sometimes hard up, felt any pressure to pursue material goals by more than a simple request for a modest increase in an extremely modest salary or a temporary honorarium. With little material ambition and with Evelyn's support Frank could devote his energy to his vocation. Not having any children in the household must have helped.

But even the explanations of passion and lack of interest in material reward may not be enough to explain fully the source of the energy that Frank devoted to his work.

In "The Intermediate Sex", published in 1908, Edward Carpenter describes typical attributes of what he describes as:

"the more normal type of Uranian (homosexual) man ... who, while possessing thoroughly masculine powers of mind and body, combines with them the tenderer and more emotional soul-nature of the woman - and sometimes to a remarkable degree. Such men, as said, are often muscular and well-built, and not distinguishable in exterior structure and the carriage of body from others of their own sex; but emotionally they are extremely complex, tender, sensitive, pitiful and loving, 'full of storm and stress, of ferment and fluctuation' of the heart; the logical faculty may or may not, in their case, be well-developed, but intuition is always strong; like women they read characters at a glance, and know, without knowing how, what is passing in the minds of others; for nursing and waiting on the needs of others they often have a peculiar gift..."

He goes on to describe their relationship with women where:

"though not naturally inclined to 'fall in love' in this direction, such men are by their nature drawn rather near to women, and it would seem that they often feel a singular appreciation and understanding of the emotional needs and destinies of the other sex, leading in many cases to a genuine though what is called 'Platonic' friendship ..."

The psychology of sex has, no doubt, moved on but Frank would probably have been familiar with Carpenter's thinking at the time the book was written and might well have recognised much of himself in the description. Nevertheless, it seems very unlikely that he thought of himself in those terms.

Indeed, it seems clear from his references to love affairs, even if unconsummated, and his attitude to Hilda, to whom he seems to have revealed his innermost person, as far as he knew it, that he thought of himself as a normal heterosexual male.

It is true that many of his friends and supporters were women, which Carpenter suggests as a possible indication of homosexuality, but perhaps an equal number were men - from Arthur Holden on. It seems that he made friends and attracted admiration from men and women alike though there is no evidence that he had physical sexual relationship with either. As far as can be told, his strong emotional relationships were with, a very few, women.

Perhaps the most likely summing up of his sexual nature is that he was, though heterosexually oriented, not drawn strongly to physical sexual activity finding it more satisfying to use his drive on the work he felt compelled to do. This may have been the ultimate source of his energy.

*　*　*

Of course, this speculation based on evidence that is best fragmentary. If it is of interest it is only because his phenomenal achievements, given that he started with nothing but his passion, demand an explanation if one can be found. But, for whatever reason, it was the sufferings of children that affected him most strongly and he gave his whole life to them. His energy, together with his self discipline – in never regretting what he could not do – allowed him to be extraordinarily effective in what he did.

Thousands had reason to be, and were, grateful for it.

BIBLIOGRAPHY

Atkinson, Blanche   The Real Princess, illustrated by Violet
and Evelyn Holden, 1894 Innes

Carpenter, Edward   Marriage in a free society, 1894, The Labour
Press Society, 1894, 47pp

Sex - Love, and its place in a free society,
The Labour Press Society, 1894, 24pp

Woman and her place in a free society,
The Labour Press Society, 1894, 41pp

The Intermediate Sex, Unwin Brothers, 1908, 176pp

Fabian Society Tracts 1, 5, 7 to 43, Fabian Society, 1884 - 1892

Harrison, Michael Bournville: Garden Village to Model Suburb:
A History, Phillimore and Co Ltd., 288pp

Holden, Edith   The Country Diary of an Edwardian
Lady. 1977, Michael Joseph, 186pp

Taylor, Ian   The Edwardian Lady – The Story of
Edith Holden. 1980, Michael Joseph, 207pp

Unknown   The House that Jack Built, Illustrated by
Violet and Evelyn Holden, 1895, Dent & Co

White, Maurice W.   Years of Caring – The Royal Orthopaedic
Hospital. Brewin Books 282p

Wilmot, Frances &   A Breath of Fresh Air - Birmingham's
Pauline Saul Open-Air Schools 1911 –1970. 1998
Phillimore & Co Ltd.

Index

Introduction to the IHWTE Publication Series

Dr. A.I. Rees grew up with Frank Mathews and the Birmingham Society for the Care of Invalid and Nervous Children. When his mother died, he became responsible for the surviving records of the Society and Frank Mathews, and in another way for the memory and history of some remarkable pioneering visions and work in creating therapeutic environments for ill, disabled and sometimes traumatised and disturbed children, and their families.

Meeting Dr. Rees in 1992, something of that sense of innovation, significance and possibility was passed on to the Archive and Study Centre, which was then in its infancy. There it matured, and when Dr. Rees completed work on his manuscript, and brought the Frank Mathews collection to the Archive and Study Centre to be permanently looked after and made available to the public, it helped to trigger what has now become the Institute for the History and Work of Therapeutic Environments.

To give it its full title, the IHWTE "is a designated research and study centre of the University of Birmingham in partnership with the Planned Environment Therapy Trust Archive, Research and Study Centre, and based at the Planned Environment Therapy Trust, Church Lane, Toddington, Cheltenham, Glos. GL54 5DQ".

To put it into other terms, the IHWTE is a creative partnership between an archive - a holder of personal and community memory - and one of the major academic research institutions in the United Kingdom. For its part, the Planned Environment Therapy Trust Archive, Research and Study Centre is the only facility of its kind, in Britain or the world, devoted specifically to therapeutic communities and environments. The partnership is devoted to deepening our understanding of what makes for a healing environment in different eras and circumstances, and to applying that understanding to practice and policy today.

At the core of the IHWTE's work is history: the record of those who have explored these questions on our behalf in the past; the stories of what they did and how and why; and the report of their successes, their failures, and the outcomes in the lives of the children, families, and staff who were involved. It is a scientific exploration of what has worked, what does work, and why.

In this we are sometimes fortunate in having the witness of living testimony. When I interviewed 93 year old Ivy Parry in 2006, she told how Frank Mathews' intervention on her behalf almost ninety years earlier, when she was diagnosed with bone tuberculosis ("Childhood's Most Dangerous Enemy" according to an 1897 article in the New York Times), had freed her from the conventional future of potential amputation, and limitation. She had grown up, married, played tennis, had children – and proved in her 20th and 21st century life, and well after he had died, the fundamental rightness of Frank Mathews' pioneering Edwardian vision.

Sometimes we are fortunate in having the evidence of direct archival memory: the original letters, logbooks and other documents produced as the raw material of the working/living day, and often thrown away at the end of it. Produced in anticipation, but in innocence of how it all turned out in the end, they allow us to reconstruct the rich and hidden grammar of the everyday discovery and problem-solving which got us to where we are now. This in turn – and especially with the amplification and clarification of living memory - gives us the potential to know ourselves better, to understand the most likely outcomes and consequences of this or that action, and to take decisions which more frequently and more accurately achieve what we want them to achieve. This is as true of a child care worker faced with an enraged child barricading themselves in a room and throwing furniture out of the window as it is a member of Parliament working in subcommittee on a new piece of social health care legislation.

But this requires that the memory is available on the one hand, and that it is robustly and energetically engaged in the present on the other. Hence this new publication series, and the Institute for the History and Work of Therapeutic Environments.

This book is the first fruit of a programme of publication which Dr. Rees helped to set in train when he brought the manuscript to the Archive and Study Centre in 2006. It contains experience and achievement which not only inform how we live and work with children and families now, but challenges any complacency we might be inclined to feel, either about ourselves and what we have achieved, or about the relative wisdom of past and present and who can learn most from listening to whom. It is the first of a series of original monographs of biography and autobiography, of unpublished archive material, of ephemeral or hard-to-find published work, of previously unpublished texts and other items which will individually and as a collection challenge our complacency, excite our imagination, and add significantly to our understanding of ourselves and our capacity to shape the future.

Dr. Craig Fees, RMSA
Honorary Director, Institute for the History and Work of Therapeutic Environments
Archivist, Planned Environment Therapy Trust Archive and Study Centre.